T H E

Life Cycle

Completed

EXTENDED VERSION

BY ERIK H. ERIKSON

Childhood and Society (1950, 1963)

Young Man Luther (1958)

Insight and Responsibility (1964)

Identity: Youth and Crisis (1968)

Gandhi's Truth (1969)

Dimensions of a New Identity (1974)

Life History and the Historical Moment (1975)

Toys and Reasons (1977)

Identity and the Life Cycle (1959, 1980)

The Life Cycle Completed (1982)

Vital Involvement in Old Age (with Joan M. Erikson and Helen Q. Kivnick) (1986)

A Way of Looking at Things: Selected Papers from 1930 to 1980 (edited by Stephen Schlein, Ph.D.) (1987)

EDITED BY ERIK H. ERIKSON

Adulthood (1978)

BY JOAN M. ERIKSON

Legacies: Prometheus-Orpheus-Socrates

The Universal Bead

St. Francis and His Four Ladies

Activity, Recovery, Growth

Wisdom and the Senses

ERIK H. ERIKSON

THE
Life Cycle
Completed

Extended Version
with New Chapters on the Ninth Stage of Development
by Joan M. Erikson

W·W·NORTON & COMPANY

New York · London

For information about permission to reproduce selections from this book,
write to Permissions,
W. W. Norton & Company, Inc., 500 Fifth Avenue, New York, NY 10110.

The text of this book is composed in 11/13 Janson
with the display set in Deepdene
Manufacturing by the Haddon Craftsmen, Inc.

Library of Congress Cataloging-in-Publication Data

Erikson, Erik H. (Erik Homburger), 1902–1994
The life cycle completed : a review / Erik H. Erikson. — Extended
version / with new chapters by Joan M. Erikson.
p. cm.
Includes bibliographical references.
ISBN 0-393-03934-X
1. Developmental psychology. 2. Psychoanalysis. 3. Personality.
I. Erikson, Joan M. (Joan Mowat) II. Title.
BF713.E73 1997
155—dc20   96-34622
                                                                         CIP

ISBN 0-393-31772-2 pbk.

W. W. Norton & Company, Inc., 500 Fifth Avenue, New York, N.Y. 10110
http://www.wwnorton.com

W. W. Norton & Company Ltd., 10 Coptic Street, London WC1A 1PU

1 2 3 4 5 6 7 8 9 0

Contents

Contents

Preface to the Extended Version

This extended version of *The Life Cycle Completed* goes beyond the earlier edition in setting forth the elements of a ninth stage of the life cycle, a stage not anticipated in the original Eriksonian approach to psychosocial development. The discussion of this new material calls for some autobiographical commentary focusing on the eighth stage, which was the final stage in the original edition of *The Life Cycle Completed*.

Before embarking on a statement about the eighth stage of the life cycle as Erik and I have understood and presented it, I would like to share with you the story of its "promotion" to stage eight.

In the late 1940s we, then living in California, received an invitation to present a paper on the developmental stages of life at the Midcentury White House Conference on Children and Youth. The paper we were to contribute for the conference was "Growth and Crises of the Healthy Personality."

We went to work with great enthusiasm. Erik had been involved in the practice of child analysis for a number of years and was in California because of his work with the Long-range Research Project on Children at the University of California at Berkeley. I was involved in raising three small children and running a household. We were sure we knew intimately about the early stages of development and were daily more aware of the problems and challenges of mid-life, marriage, and parenting. It is amazing how informed one can feel in the midst of the demands of such a tangled warp of undigested relationships.

With a neat plot of squares and carefully selected words, the whole life cycle could be presented on one sheet of paper. Many of the future refinements and elaborations were not indicated in any way. Later this chart was to grow in length and girth and would be woven in dramatic color. I have always contended that the life cycle chart becomes really meaningful only when you have observed it as a weaving or, even better, have undertaken to weave it yourself.

Shortly before the White House conference, Erik was invited to present the "stages" to a group of psychologists and psychiatrists in Los Angeles. Such an assignment seemed to offer a good opportunity to discuss and test out this material. The plan was for us to drive to the nearest train station, where Erik could catch the Los Angeles train, and then for me to hurry back to home and the children.

It was a fairly long drive from the Berkeley hills to the train station in South San Francisco, and we used the time to discuss the chart and its presentation. We also were delighted to remember that when the great Shakespeare had written his "Seven Ages of Man," he had entirely neglected to include—of all things—the play stage, stage three in our more inclusive model. What a fascinating paradox! Perhaps it was blindness on his part to the role of play in the lives of every child and adult. We felt amused and very wise.

Let me recall for you a few things the illustrious Bard had to say about the ages of man. The prospect of aging for men was gloomy indeed.

> *All the world's a stage,*
> *And all the men and women merely players:*
> *They have their exits and their entrances;*
> *And one man in his time plays many parts,*
> *His acts being seven ages. At first the infant,*
> *Mewling and puking in the nurse's arms.*
> *And then the whining school-boy, with his satchel*

And shining morning face, creeping like snail
Unwillingly to school. And then the lover,
Sighing like furnace, with a woeful ballad
Made to his mistress' eyebrow. Then a soldier,
Full of strange oaths and bearded like the pard,
Jealous in honour, sudden and quick in quarrel,
Seeking the bubble reputation
Even in the cannon's mouth. And then the justice,
In fair round belly with good capon lined,
With eyes severe and beard of formal cut,
Full of wise saws and modern instances;
And so he plays his part. The sixth age shifts
Into the lean and slipper'd pantaloon,
With spectacles on nose and pouch on side,
His youthful hose, well saved, a world too wide
For his shrunk shank; and his big manly voice,
Turning again toward childish treble, pipes
And whistles in his sound. Last scene of all,
That ends this strange eventful history,
Is second childishness and mere oblivion,
Sans teeth, sans eyes, sans taste, sans every thing.

—As You Like It, act II, Scene 7, 139

Sitting with the life cycle chart on my lap while Erik drove, I began to feel uneasy. Shakespeare had seven stages, as did we, and he had omitted an important one. Had we too left one out? In a shocking moment of clarity I saw what was wrong: "We" were missing, and so were the children and Erik's new book *Children and Society*. The seven chart stages jumped from "Intimacy" (stage six) to "Old Age" (stage seven). We surely needed another stage between the sixth and seventh, but time was short. Soon we included a new seventh stage entitled "Generativity vs. Stagnation," followed by "Old Age" with the strengths of wisdom and integrity promoted to the eighth stage.

How difficult it is to recognize and have perspective for just where one is presently in one's own life cycle. Today is like yesterday until you sit back and take stock. Would we recognize old age as it crept up and the days rushed on? Only very slowly did we begin to learn the particulars of the eighth stage.

THE EIGHTH STAGE

Having come to terms with generativity in time for the White House conference, we found much to keep us busy with the growing-up needs of the children, travel and research grants, and many other pursuits. Although some energy slowly dissipated, we kept steaming along until old age really began to make itself felt. Probably we had been sliding downhill for quite some time, but we didn't take it seriously, and our friends supported our unconcern.

When Erik wrote *The Life Cycle Completed,* his ninth decade had not yet begun. Although at age eighty we began to acknowledge our elderly status, I believe we never faced its challenges realistically until we were close to ninety. Our lives had not been beset with unresolvable difficulties. At ninety we woke up in foreign territory. Whatever premonitions we may have encountered earlier and tossed off as odd and even funny, we soon began to face unavoidable—and certainly not amusing—realities.

As we had passed through the years of generativity, it had never felt as though the end of the road were here and now. We had still taken years ahead for granted. At ninety the vistas changed; the view ahead became limited and unclear. Death's door, which we always knew was expectable but had taken in stride, now seemed just down the block.

When Erik was ninety-one, he and I had been married for sixty-four years. Following hip surgery, he became withdrawn, and he serenely retired. He was neither depressed nor bewildered but remained consistently observing and quietly appreciative of his caretakers. We should all be so wise, gracious, and accepting of old age when it comes our way. I am now ninety-three years old and have experienced more of the inevitable complications of *slowly* growing old. I am not retired, serene, and gracious. In fact I am eager to finish this revision of the final stage before it is too late and too demanding an undertaking.

After the publication of *The Life Cycle Completed* in 1982, Erik reread it critically, underlining and annotating it unsparingly from cover to cover with red, black, and blue ink. I checked his own copy, and that only by chance, shortly before his death. no page is free of his underlining, exclamation marks, and notes. Only an artist would be so daring and forthright.

Erik, who was meticulous about his writing, found it necessary to mark up with criticisms every page of the published book, and I found myself wondering what he was trying to tell me. In what way did these firm annotations revise our previous thinking and add to our understanding of the life cycle.

My purpose in reviewing the eighth stage of our life cycle chart, and the strengths attributed to it, is to clarify several meaningful and important discrepancies, now that Erik and I have "arrived," so to speak. My comments are written in the light of both Erik's statement that a review of "our attempt to complete the life cycle in our life time seemed indeed appropriate and justifiable."* In the early 1940s, when we were searching for the most accurate words to designate the life cycle virtues, we selected "wisdom" and "integrity" as the final strengths to come to full maturity in old age. We had initially considered "hope" because it was mandatory for survival and was needed for all other strengths. But since hope becomes vital from infancy on, it clearly does not demand time for its fruition even though it may endure throughout life. Having named wisdom and integrity as the strengths of old age, we were now challenged to justify this selection.

"Wisdom" and "integrity" are among those high-sounding words that have been personified, cast in bronze, carved in stone and wood. When one considers such virtues or strengths, one is apt to be reminded of imposing statues created to portray the characteristics that such words imply: sky-gazing Liberty, who holds a torch; Justice, eyes bound, with a scale in hand; and omnipresent Faith, Hope, and Charity. We extol them in silence in stone, plaster, and metal and revere them with high-minded respect.

I believe that the relationship of elders to the words "wisdom" and "integrity" is entirely askew unless we first understand the earthbound strength of these attributes. These virtues have become too

* *The Life Cycle Completed,* p. 9.

exalted and undefinable. We need to bring them down to actuality. We must wring their true meaning out of them. Surely, for example, wisdom is not adequately represented by volumes of thoughtful information, overloaded with facts and formulas. Definitions provided by a college dictionary (Random House) are equally inadequate: "Quality or state of being wise; knowledge of what is true and right coupled with good judgment; scholarly knowledge or learning; wise sayings or teachings."

We must dig down to the roots, to the very seed, of "wisdom" and "integrity." The *Oxford English Dictionary* relentlessly boils words down, offering us old and valid earthbound connections. After six inches of tiny print we arrive at *the word*, the mother lodestone or kernel of illustrious "wisdom." This small root is *vēda* "to see, to know."

This word *vēda* takes us back to the ancient, hallowed myths and mysterious messages of the sacred Sanskrit writings of India, collectively named the Vedas. The Vedas incorporate the eternal quest for vision understanding and wisdom. The sris first saw the Vedas; wisdom, illumination were transmitted by sight.

We take the wonderful gift of sight for granted unless or until it no longer consistently serves us as we might expect and wish. We can look back over a long past, and so doing helps us understand our lives and the world we live in. We look forward, and this looking may be merely wishful thinking or hopeful dreaming, but without the promising prospect of the future, all might be dulled with apprehension. In blithe American fashion, however, we have latched on to a phrase that exemplifies a slangy acceptance of the ancient wisdom. How smart we are in our ignorance when we casually say, "Oh, I see. I get it. I understand." We do, however, have high respect and appreciation for such words as "enlightenment," "discernment," and "insight," all related to seeing and vision.

It is so painful for those of us gifted with sight to consider what life without it would mean that we tend to avoid such speculation. Those not so endowed probably develop to a high degree their capacities to hear, smell, taste, and touch. Who knows how enriched they may be by the extension and clarity of these other senses? Perhaps they think that our overdependence on sight actually deprives us. Alert vision orients and integrates us with the earth where we live and move, find sustenance, and learn how to get along with other people, animals, and nature. For this the eyes must be wide open and alert. For this also the ear must be set to take advantage of all signals and understand their meaning.

Having responded with delight to the root meaning of the word *wisdom*, I made a further discovery. Thousands of years ago the word for "ear" and for "wisdom" in the Sumerian language seems to have been one and the same. This word was probably "enki," since the god of wisdom in Sumer was addressed by this name. "From the Great Above the goddess opened [set] her ear, her receptor for wisdom, to the Great Below."* If wisdom is conveyed through sound as well as sight, then singing, rhythmic gesture, and dance are included as its conveyors and amplifiers. Sound is powerful; sound can soothe, enlighten, inform, and stimulate. It challenges us with its potential, and we are dependent on our aural perception for the development of wisdom.

Now we can see that wisdom belongs to the world of actuality to which our senses give us access. So it is with our senses that we understand   through sight and hearing, enriched and supported as they are by scent, taste, and touch   for all animals have these gifts and attributes. These invaluable sources of information do not necessarily improve in their functioning over time, but the alert mind will retain the information wisely stored for use as the need arises. It is also the role of wisdom to guide our investment in sight and sound and to focus our capacities on what is relevant, enduring, and nourishing, both for us individually and for the society in which we live.

We have designated a second attribute to elders that is as lofty and exalted as wisdom and even less understood. Rather than risk the confusion of identifying its meaning with exalted representations of it as an attribute of a person immortalized/memorialized in statues, we do well to look again for its pithiest meaning in the *OED*.

* Diane Wolkstein and Samuel Noah Kramer, *Innana, Queen of Heaven and Earth* (New York: Harper & Row, 1983, pp. 155–56).

The long three- or four-inch paragraph of word parts out of which the word "integrity" grows ends with the surprising root word "tact." From this element we derive "contact," "intact," "tactile," "tangible," "tack," even "touch." It is with our bodies, our senses that we construct edifices, fashion materials, and respond to the intimations of the holy, the powerful, and the wise messages of earth and the heavens. It is in actuality that we live and move and share the earth with one another. Without contact there is no growth; in fact without contact life is not possible. Independence is a fallacy.

To understand integrity in these terms makes all those mute and immobilized statues come to life. If we consider integrity merely a noble ideal to be embroidered on a banner and raised high in appropriate situations, we would be doing it a grave injustice. Integrity has the function of promoting contact with the world, with things, and, above all, with people. It is a tactile and a tangible way to live, not an intangible, virtuous goal to seek after and achieve. When we say the clause "This person's work has integrity," we offer the highest praise because the work demonstrates its capacity to hold together. It is sturdy and reliable, not ethereal. It is a confirmation of sight and sound and skill involving all our senses.

Integrity is a wonderfully challenging word. It demands no strenuous deliberation or performance, just everyday management of all major and minor activities, with all the steadfast attention to detail necessary for a day well lived. It is all so simple, so direct, and so difficult.

Now that we more fully understand the implications of the term "integrity," what does it offer to those at the eighth stage of the life cycle? For one thing, whereas formerly it shone like a starry virtue in the sky, it now is a consistently close element in our daily, very earthy life. It stretches our being into contact with the real, surrounding world: with light, sound, smell, and in touch with all animate beings. Everybody, everything matters intensely, more than ever before. Every meeting takes on a special meaning, offers enrichment, or points in an unexpected and rewarding direction.

As I consider these revised, but much more ancient, meanings of the words "integrity" and "wisdom," I am released and relieved of the onerous, rather vague, responsibility of a long life of strictures on action or stance. To accept the promise that these new interpretations offer old age is to unfold a vista of the past that is radiant and exhilarating. Love, devotion, and friendship bloom; sadness is tender and enriching; the beauty of relationships is deeply heartwarming. Looking back is engagingly memorable; the present is natural and full of little pleasures, immense joys, and much laughter.

Whereas initially the words "wisdom" and "integrity" seemed a burdensome challenge to elders, the same words, now clearly understood, reinstate their appropriateness. What is demanded is the aliveness and awareness that it takes to live with tact and vision in all relationships. One must join in the process of adaptation. With whatever tact and wisdom we can muster, disabilities must be accepted with lightness and humor. We all have taken our youthful capacities for granted and enjoyed them hugely. Let us applaud the performers now with tact and true appreciation. With hearing and sight we are privileged; keep on looking and listening.

Old age demands that one garner and lean on all previous experience, maintaining awareness and creativity with a new grace. There is often something one might call indomitable about many old people. Erik has called it an "invariable core," the "existential identity," that is an integration of past, present, and future. It transcends the self and underscores the presence of intergenerational links. It is universal in its acceptance of the human condition. Part of the human condition is to lack wisdom about ourselves and our planet. We must become aware of how little we know. Perhaps we could wisely "become like little children" who are willing to live, love, and learn openly. What does that imply? Life has been rich. Trust it further like a trusting child. Relax and try to be unselfconsciously playful. Whenever you have playmates, play and let it take you with laughter where you haven't been for years!

Thus we submit that wisdom and integrity are active, lifelong developing processes, as are all the strengths included in the life cycle stages. They are definitely ongoing, should we dare to hope contagious, unending, perhaps everlasting?

Preface to the First Edition

This monograph is based on an essay that the National Institute of Mental Health asked me to contribute to their three-volume *The Course of Life, Psychoanalytic Contributions Toward Understanding Personality Development*. There, it is the second of two introductory chapters invited by the editors, S. I. Greenspan and G. H. Pollock (1980). The first was written by Anna Freud and occupied exactly ten modest and thoroughly clear pages—to my fifty. Her introduction carries the title "Child Analysis as the Study of Mental Growth (Normal and Abnormal)" and begins with the original child-analytic work done in Vienna, Berlin, and London. A special section summarizes the function of the *Developmental Lines*, a conceptual scheme designed by Anna Freud and the staff of the Hampstead Clinic (A. Freud 1963). These "lines" lead from infantile immaturity to the reliable (and yet conflictual) categories of behavior expected from the "average adult." Here are some examples: "from libidinal dependence to self-reliance"; "from ego centricity to peer relationships"; "from play to work." As a concept, this developmental scheme is, of course, based on the two fundamental theories of psychoanalysis; namely, that of *psychosexual development* and of the *ego*.

My contribution (1980(a)) attempted to outline the "elements" of a *psychoanalytic* theory of *psychosocial* development. I, too, first traced the gradual inclusion in psychoanalytic thought of what was once called "the outerworld" back to my last days of psychoanalytic training in Vienna and on through my first years in this country. Having emphasized the complementarity of psychosexual and psychosocial approaches and their relation to the concept of ego, I proceeded to review the corresponding stages of the life cycle.

Now to restate at such length what theoretical considerations one has advanced in a lifetime and in a variety of data-filled contexts may seem to be an unrewarding task to writer and reader alike. But it was, in fact, the historical emphasis of the invitation from the NIMH that to me seemed to suggest it as a valid undertaking: for such an extension of psychoanalytic theory could have originated only in this country and in a period—the thirties and forties—when psychoanalysis, against a background of growing world turbulence, found itself welcomed into medical centers as well as into intensive interdisciplinary discussion. And such discussions later proved to be fundamental to the central theme of the Midcentury White House Conference on Children and Youth to which Joan Erikson and I contributed a paper, "Growth and Crises of the 'Healthy Personality' " (1950).

So, I decided to republish and, where necessary, to extend what I had written for the NIMH—and this with only one major change; when it came (once more!) to a review of the stages of life, I changed the order of my presentation. Already in the NIMH chapter, I had elected to begin the list of the psychosocial stages not, as is customary, with childhood, but with *adulthood:* the "idea" being that once you have worked out the interweaving of all the stages you should be able to start with any stage and—meaningfully—reach any other on the map of stages. And adulthood, after all, *is* the link between the individual life cycle and the cycle of generations. In this essay, however, I go further and begin my account of the stages with the last one, *old age*, to see how much sense a re-view of the *completed* life cycle can make of its whole course.

Wherever we begin, however, the central role that the stages of life are playing in our psychosocial theorizing will lead us ever deeper into the issues of *historical relativity*. Thus, a look back on this century's last few decades makes it clear that *old age* was "discovered" only in recent years—and this both for theoretical and historical reasons—for it certainly demanded some redefinition when an ever-increasing number of old people were found (and found themselves) to represent a mass of *elderlies* rather than an elite of *elders*. Before that, however, we had come at last to acknowledge *adulthood* as a developmental and conflictual phase in its own right, rather than merely the mature end of all development (i.e., Benedek 1959). Before *that* (and then only in the sixties, a period of national identity crisis dramatically reflected in the public behavior of some of our youth), we had learned to pay full attention to the adolescent *identity crisis* as central to the developmental dynamics of the life cycle (Erikson 1959). And as pointed out, it had not been before the midcentury that the child's "healthy personality" and all the infantile stages discovered only in this century really became the center of systematic national attention.

In reading this essay, then, the reader—in his or her life-historical time and place—may wish to review our attempt to "complete" the life cycle in our lifetime. It is hoped that this title sounds just ironic enough not to be taken as a promise of an all-inclusive accounting of a perfect human life. For it is intended to confirm only the fact that if one speaks of life as a cycle, one has already implied some kind of self-completion. But how one elaborates on this at a given time depends, of course, on the theoretical stage of one's field and on the significance that different periods of life then happen to have for ourselves and for our fellow men. Today, do some of our terms and concepts seem all too timebound—or agebound? And if changes are suggested by changing times, can our terms retain their original significance and continue to contribute to each other's meaning?

I myself can only restate the terms here as they "occurred" to us in their then suggestive, but also fairly orderly, complexity: a complexity, however, that promptly invited lasting misunderstandings. In restating them here I cannot avoid arousing in some of my readers the repeated suspicion that they "somewhere" have already read this or that, maybe longish, passage. They most probably have: for in this summary it has seemed to me here and there pointless to rephrase what seems already to have been rather fittingly formulated.

It so happens that my *acknowledgments* can also be offered in terms of a sequence of decades. What I have learned from coworkers can best be noted by listing those research institutions that I had the privilege to be associated with while practicing psychoanalysis and taking part in its applications in medical schools. In the 1930s, I was affiliated with the Harvard Psychological Clinic and the Yale Institute of Human Relations; in the forties, with the Guidance Study in the Institute of Human Development at the University of California, Berkeley; and in the fifties, with the residential Austen Riggs Center in the Berkshires. Each of these, with its innovative ways, permitted me to become involved unforgettably in the clinical or developmental study of given age groups of human beings. In the sixties, finally, my own undergraduate course on "The Human Life Cycle," at Harvard, permitted me to share the developing scheme with a large group of responsive students intensely interested in life as well as in history.

Some individuals whose support was especially vital over the years are named in the text. Any attempt to do them (and unnamed others) "justice" in this context would seem futile.[1]

As in all my prefaces, I conclude my acknowledgments with

[1] The work on this essay was in part supported by a grant from the Maurice Falk Medical Fund in Pittsburgh, Pennsylvania.

my thanks to Joan Erikson. Our (just mentioned) joint contribution to the Midcentury White House Conference makes it especially clear that her "editorial" guidance has always gone way beyond an attempt to make me readable: it has enlivened the whole imagery of the life cycle reviewed here (J. Erikson 1950, 1976).

1

Introduction

A HISTORICAL NOTE ON THE "OUTERWORLD"

THE TERM AND CONCEPT, "psychosocial," in a psychoanalytic context, is obviously meant to complement the dominant theory of psychosexuality. To chart the beginnings of such an effort I must go back to the time of my training in Vienna—the period of ascendance of ego psychology—and briefly trace some changing conceptualizations of the ego's relation to the social environment. True, the two basic works on the ego,—Anna Freud's *The Ego and the Mechanisms of Defence* and H. Hartmann's *Ego Psychology and the Problem of Adaptation*—appeared only in 1936 and in 1939, respectively. But the observations and conclusions on which these two works were based dominated much of the discussion in the years before the completion of my training and my migration to the United States in 1933. The defensive and the adaptive functions of the ego have, in the meantime, become firm facets of psychoanalytic theory. My purpose in referring back to their origins is to indicate in what way, to a young worker, the overall theory seemed to be working toward and yet stopping short of a systematic attention to the ego's role in the relationship of *individuality* and *communality*.

Most interesting in retrospect and most indicative of the hidden ideological controversies that mark the advancement of a field was the original discord between A. Freud's and Hartmann's emerging ideas. Anna Freud herself, in her straightforward way, reports that when she first formally submitted her conclusions regarding the defensive functions of the ego to the Vienna Society in 1936, "Hartmann showed himself appreciative on the whole, but he emphasized the point that to show the ego at war with the id was not the whole story, that there were many additional problems of ego growth and ego functioning which needed consideration. My views were more restricted at the time, and this was news to me which I was not yet ready to assimilate." For, she continues, her contribution came "from the side of the ego's defensive activity against the drives; Hartmann's, in a more revolutionary manner, from the new angle of ego autonomy which until then had lain outside analytic study" (Loewenstein et al. 1966).

The last three words, as well as the designation "revolutionary," point to the question of self-chosen boundaries drawn at various times in the development of psychoanalytic theory. To appreciate these, we would need to consider the ideological as well as the scientific implications of every advance and of every corresponding term in psychoanalytic theory, and, indeed, in all applications of theories of natural science to man. Freud's original position, of course, was *drive* oriented, and my generation of men and women trained in Middle Europe will remember that this most fundamental of all terms, *Trieb*, in its German usage had a number of nature-philosophical connotations as an ennobling as well as an upsetting force: this (for better or for worse) was lost in its translation into either "instinct" or "drive." *Die suessen Triebe*—"the sweet drives,"—the German poet could say: while stern physiologists could speak of the obligation in all work worthy of the name of science to find "forces of equal dignity"

(Jones 1953)—equal to those already isolated and quantified in the natural sciences. But if Freud insisted that "all our provisional ideas in psychology will presumably some day be based on an organic substructure" (1914), he also made it clear that he was willing to wait for a truly reliable experimental substantiation of an all-inclusive and then still admittedly mythical *instinctual energy*. Thus we learned that he was opposed to Reich's "materialistic" attempts to find measurable traces of libido in the tonus of some body surfaces.

Freud's work had begun in the century of Darwin's search for the evolutionary origin of the species; and the new humanist ethos demanded that mankind, once so proud of the consciousness and the moral stature of its assumed civilized maturity, would have to accept the discovery of its primary roots in its animal ancestry, in its own primeval prehistory, and in the infantile stages of ontogeny. All this, at any rate, was once implied in that terminology of instinctual energy that over the years has come to convey a certain ritualistic conviction rather than the persistent hope of strict scientific substantiation. In its time, however, that energetic form of thought opened up undreamt-of—or was it dreamt-of—insights. The purpose of drawing his line there, however, was (as the recently published correspondence between Freud and Jung has again so dramatically illustrated) Freud's conviction of the prime necessity to study vigilantly that unconscious and instinctual core of man which he called the "id" (and thus something akin to an inner outerworld) and to take no chances with mankind's tenacious resistance to insights into its "lower" nature, and its tendency to devitalize such insights by remythologizing them as "higher." No wonder, then, that social reality, in relation to the inner cauldron to be explored, at first occupied something of an extraterritorial position and, more often than not, was referred to as the "outer-world" or "external reality." Thus, our proud ego, which Freud called a "frontier creature," "owes service to three masters and is consequently menaced by three dangers: from the external world, from the libido of the id, and from the severity of the super-ego" (S. Freud 1923).

When first discussing the relationship of the ego to group life, Freud (1921) discussed those social authors of his time (for example, Le Bon, McDougal) who elaborated on "artificial" group formations—that is, mobs, crowds, mere masses, or what Freud calls "primary" and "primitive" groups. He focused on the "grownup individual's *insertion* into a collection of people which has *acquired* the characteristic of a psychological group" (italics mine). Prophetically, he mused on how such groups "allow man to throw off the repression of his unconscious impulses." Freud did not, at that time, ask the fundamental question as to how the individual had ever acquired what he "possessed outside the primitive group"; namely, *"his own continuity, his self-consciousness, his traditions, and his customs, his own particular functions and position."* Freud's main objective in analyzing "artificial" groups (such as a church or an army) was to show that such groups are held together by "love instincts" which have been diverted from their biological aims to help form social attachments, "though they do not operate with less energy on that account." This last assumption must interest us in the context of psychosocial development: By what lawfulness can "love be transferred . . . from sexual *to social* aims"—transferred undiminished?

Anna Freud, in her summary of the ego's defensive measures, again relegated the otherwise acknowledged presence of social forces to an "outside world": "The ego is victorious when its defensive measures enable it to restrict the development of anxiety and so to transform the instincts that, even in difficult circumstances, some measure of gratification is secured, thereby establishing the most harmonious relations possible between the id, the super-ego, and the forces of the outside world" (A. Freud 1936). In her later work, this trend continued in the formulation of the *developmental lines* that "in every instance . . . trace the child's gradual outgrowing of dependent, irrational, id- and object-determined attitudes to an increasing ego mastery of his internal and external world" (A. Freud 1965). In asking, however, "what singles out individual lines for special promotion in development," Anna Freud did suggest that "we have to look to accidental environmental influences. In the analysis of older children and the reconstruction from adult analysis we have found these forces embodied in the parents' personalities, their actions and ideals, the family atmosphere, the impact of the cultural setting as a whole." Here the question remains which of these environmental influences are more or less "accidental."

Hartmann, in turn, went all out in suggesting that the human ego, far from being merely evolution's defense against the id, had independent roots. He, in fact, called such classical functions of the human mind as motility, perception, and memory "ego apparatuses of primary autonomy." He also considered all these developing capacities to be in a state of adaptedness to what he called "an average expectable environment." As Rapaport put it: "By means of these concepts [he] laid the foundation for the psychoanalytic concept and theory of adaptation, and outlined the first generalized theory of *reality relations* in psychoanalytic ego psychology" (Rapaport in Erikson 1959). But, Rapaport adds, he "does not provide a specific and differentiated psychosocial theory." And, indeed, an "average expectable environment" seems to postulate only a minimum of those conditions that, one is tempted to say, may make mere survival possible, but it seems to ignore the enormous variations and complexities of social life that are the source of individual and communal vitality—as well as dramatic conflict. In fact, Hartmann's writings, too, continued to employ such terms as "acting in regard to reality," "action vis-a-vis reality" (1947) and "acting in the outer world" (1956), to mention only some of the shortest quotable indications as to where, in a field's development, the lines may be drawn at a given time.

The mechanistic and physicalistic wording of psychoanalytic theory, as well as the persistent references to the "outerworld," came to puzzle me early in my training, and this especially in view of the general climate of the *clinical* seminars,—Anna Freud's "Kinderseminar" in particular—that were alive with a new closeness to social as well as inner problems and were thus animated by a spirit that characterizes the nature of psychoanalytic training at its best. Freud once wrote to Romain Rolland that "our inborn instincts and the world around us being what they are, I could not but regard that love as no less essential for the survival of the human race than such things as technology" (1926). And we students could, indeed, experience in clinical discussions a modern form of caritas in the acknowledgement that, in principle, all human beings are equal in their exposure to the same conflicts and that the psychoanalytic "technique" demands the psychoanalyst's insight into the conflicts he may inescapably (and most instructively) be "transferring" from his own life to a given therapeutic situation.

These are, at any rate, the concepts and words I would use today to characterize the core of a new communal spirit that I perceived at times in my student years. Thus, the extensive, and intensive, presentation and discussion of cases seemed to be in polar contrast to the terminological legacy that provided the framework for theoretical discourse. The *clinical* and the *theoretical* language seemed to celebrate two different attitudes toward human motivation, although they proved complementary to each other within our training experience.

Furthermore, as the treatment of adults had led to the formulation of some definite and most fateful substages of childhood, and thus to developmental assumptions that set an early pattern for the eventual study of the whole life cycle, the direct psychoanalytic observation and treatment of children had suggested itself powerfully. In the discussion of such work, the *developmental ethos* of psychoanalysis came to manifest itself most clearly, for as children offered striking symptomatic verifications of the pathographic assumptions of psychoanalysis, they often did so by outdoing all adult expectations in their directness of playful and communicative expression. Thus, they revealed, along with the child's intense conflicts, a resourceful and inventive striving for experience and synthesis. It was in the seminars dealing with child patients and shared by psychoanalysts deeply involved in "progressive education" that the reductionist language of scientistic theory moved into the background, while the foreground became vivid with innumerable details illustrating the patient's mutual involvement with significant persons. Here, instead of the single person's inner "economics" of drive and defense, an *ecology* of mutual activation within a communal unit such as the family suggested itself as a future subject of study. This seemed particularly true for the observations reported by the two leading observers of youth, Siegfried Bernfeld and August Aichhorn. The first I learned to know primarily as a great visiting speaker and the second as the most empathic and down-to-earth discussant of individual young delinquents.

Today, I would not hesitate to designate the basic difference between the theoretical and the clinical approaches characterizing our training as that between last century's preoccupation with the economics of energy and this century's emphasis on complementarity and relativity. Without quite knowing what I was doing, I later titled the first chapter of my first book "Relevance and Relativity in the Case History" (1951, 1963). Whatever I said there, and however analogistic such thinking may be, I have come to consider the basic clinical attitude of psychoanalysis an experience based on the acknowledgment of multiple relativities—which I hope will become clear in this essay.

But there was a third ingredient in the training situation in Vienna that to me could not be subordinated to either the clinical or theoretical approach: I mean the pleasure (I can only call it aesthetic) of an open, *configurational attention* to the rich interplay of form and meaning, for which, above all, Freud's *Interpretation of Dreams* was the model. From there it was easily transferred to the observation of children's play behavior and permitted equal attention to what such behavior denied and distorted and to that (often humorous) artfulness of manifest expression, without which symbolic, ritualized, and, indeed, ritual patterns of behavior could not be understood—and without which I, as one then trained more in visual than in verbal communication, could not have found a "natural" access to such overwhelming data. (At any rate, one of my first psychoanalytic papers in Vienna was on children's picture books [1931], and my first paper in this country was to be "Configurations in Play" [1937]). I reiterate all this here because to me these ingredients remain basic for the art-and-science of psychoanalysis and cannot be replaced for the purpose of "proof" by experimental and statistical investigations, suggestive and satisfying as they may be in their own right.

But it is high time that I mention the dominant fact that the historical period in which we learned to observe such revelations of the inner life was well on its way to turning into one of the most catastrophic periods in history; and the ideological division between the "inner-" and the "outerworld" may well have had deep connotations of a threatening split between the individualistic enlightenment rooted in Judaeo-Christian civilization and the totalitarian veneration of the racist state. This fact was about to threaten the very lives of some of those then engaged in the studies described here. Yet, their efforts were (as the quoted publication dates show) stubbornly redoubled, as if a methodical devotion to the timeless pursuits of healing and enlightenment was now needed all the more desperately.

In the meantime, on this side of the Atlantic even younger psychoanalysts like myself found that the cautious but definite pointers toward social inquiry prepared in the development of Viennese ego psychology could be immediately continued and expanded, as we were drawn eagerly into interdisciplinary work and shared the pioneer spirit of new psychoanalytic institutes as well as of new "schools." At Harvard, there was a hospitable medical milieu invigorated by upsurging psychiatric social work. There also Henry A. Murry was studying life histories rather than case histories; while at a variety of interdisciplinary meetings (under the wide influence of Lawrence K. Frank, Margaret

Mead, and others), the doors between the different compartments of medical and social study were unlocked for an exchange of concerns that soon proved complementary. And so it happened that in the very year when *The Ego and the Mechanisms of Defence* (A. Freud 1936) appeared in Vienna, I was privileged to accompany the anthropologist Scudder Mekeel to the Sioux Indians' reservation at Pine Ridge in South Dakota and could make observations that proved basic to a psychoanalytic, psychosocial theory. One of the most surprising features in our first conversations with American Indians was the convergence between the rationale given by the Indians for their ancient methods of childrearing and the psychoanalytic reasoning by which we would come to consider the same data relevant and interdependent. Training in such groups, so we soon concluded, is the method by which a group's basic ways of organizing experience (its group ethos, as we came to call it) is transmitted to the infant's early bodily experiences and, through them, to the beginnings of his ego.

The comparative reconstruction of the ancient child-training systems of this hunting tribe of the Great Plains, and, later, of a California fishing tribe, threw much light on what Spitz called the "dialogue" between the child's developmental readiness and the pattern of maternal care readied for the child by a community—"the source and origin of species-specific adaptation" (Spitz 1963, p. 174). We also learned to recognize the importance of the style of child training not only for the inner economy of the individual life cycle but also for the ecological balance of a given community under changing *technological* and *historical* conditions.

It was no consolation then, but it provided a certain grim encouragement, that what we gradually learned of the holocaust and experienced in World War II at least suggested the future possibility of a clarification by a new political psychology of the most devastatingly destructive trends in the seemingly most civilized and advanced representatives of the human species.

It is the limited concern of this essay to clarify the psychosocial theory that evolved, especially in regard to its origins in, and its possible significance for, psychoanalytic theory as a whole. What, to begin with the beginning, *is* the function of pregenitality, that great distributor of libidinal energy, in the healthy as well as the disturbed ecology of the individual life cycle—and in the cycle of generations? Does pregenitality exist only for genitality and ego synthesis only for the individual?

What follows is based on a great variety of observations and experiences, clinical and "applied," that are related in my publications. For this time I must, as pointed out, attempt to do without narrative. Moreover, having said it all (or most) before, I must paraphrase and, here and there, even quote myself.

At the same time, I would be quite unable to relate such summary thoughts to those of others who over the decades have expressed similar or opposing views without, however, claiming to represent a psychosocial point of view within psychoanalysis. It is such a circumscribed effort that seemed warranted by the invitation of the NIMH.

2

Psychosexuality and the Cycle of Generations

EPIGENESIS AND PREGENITALITY

COMBINED DESIGNATIONS such as "psycho-sexual" and "psycho-social" are obviously meant to open the borderlines of two fields, each established in its methodological and ideological realm, for two-way traffic. But such hyphenated attempts rarely overcome the human tendency to mistake what can be submitted to established techniques for the true nature of things. Luckily, healing always calls for a holistic attitude that does not argue with established facts but, above all, attempts to include them in a wider context of some enlightening quality. On the basis of case-historical and life-historical experience, therefore, I can only begin with the assumption that a human being's existence depends at every moment on three processes of organization that must complement each other. There is, in whatever order, the biological process of the hierarchic organization of organ systems constituting a body (*soma*); there is the psychic process organizing individual experience by ego synthesis (*psyche*); and there is the communal process of the cultural organization of the interdependence of persons (*ethos*).

To begin with, each of these processes has its own specialized methods of investigation that must, in fact, stay clear of each other in order to isolate and study certain elements basic to nature and to man. But, in the end, all three approaches are necessary for the clarification of any intact human event.

In clinical work, of course, we come face to face with the often much more striking way in which these processes, by their very nature, are apt to fail and isolate each other, causing what by different methods can be studied as somatic *tension*, individual *anxiety*, or social *panic*. What makes clinical work so instructive, however, is the rule that to approach human behavior in terms of one of these processes always means to find oneself involved in the others, for each item that proves relevant in one process is seen to give significance to, as it receives meaning from, items in the others. One may—as Freud did in his clinical studies of the neuroses of his time and in accordance with the dominant scientific concepts of his period—find a decisively new access to human motivation by assuming an all-powerful sexual energy (Eros) denied by human consciousness, repressed by the dominant morality, and ignored by science. And the very magnitude, in his time, of the repression of sexuality, aggravated as it was by a massive cultural prohibition, helped to endow the theory of sexual energy first with shocked alarm and then with a glow of liberation. Yet, any exhaustive case history, life history, or historical account will lead us to consider the interplay of this hypothesized energy with energies contributed (or withheld!) by the other processes. Freud's own dream reports and case fragments, at any rate, always contain data pointing to such ecological considerations.

The *organismic principle* that in our work has proven indispensable for the somatic grounding of psychosexual and psychosocial development is *epigenesis*. This term is borrowed from embryology, and whatever its status today, in the early days of our work it advanced our understanding of the relativity governing human phenomena linked with organismic growth.

When Freud recognized infantile sexuality, sexology stood about where embryology had stood in medieval times. Even as embryology once assumed that a minute but completely formed "homunculus" was ready in the man's semen to be implanted into a woman's uterus, there to expand and from there to step into life, sexology before Freud assumed that sexuality emerged and developed during puberty without any preparatory infantile stages. Eventually, however, embryology came to understand epigenetic development, the step-by-step growth of the fetal organs, even as psychoanalysis discovered the pregenital stages of sexuality. How are the two kinds of stage development related?

As I now quote what the embryologist has to tell us about the epigenesis of organ systems, I hope that the reader will "hear" the probability that all growth and development follow analogous patterns. In the epigenetic sequence of development each organ has its time of origin—a factor as important as the locus of origin. If the eye, said Stockard, does not arise at the appointed time, "it will never be able to express itself fully, since the moment for the rapid outgrowth of some other part will have arrived" (1931). But if it has begun to arise at the right time, still another time factor determines the most critical stage of its development: "A given organ must be interrupted during the early stage of its development in order to be completely suppressed or grossly modified" (Stockard 1931). If the organ misses its time of ascendance, it is not only doomed as an entity, it endangers at the same time the whole hierarchy of organs. "Not only does the arrest of a rapidly budding part . . . tend to suppress its development temporarily, but the premature loss of supremacy to some other organ renders it impossible for the suppressed part to come again into dominance so that it is permanently modified." The result of normal development, however, is proper relationship of size and function among all body organs: the liver adjusted in size to the stomach and intestine; the heart and lungs properly balanced; and the capacity of the vascular system accurately proportioned to the body as a whole.

Embryology, too, learned much about normal development from the developmental accidents which cause "monstra in excessu" and "monstra in defectu," even as Freud was led to recognize the laws of normal infantile pregenitality from the clinical observation of the distortion of genitality either by symptoms of "excessive" perversion or of "defective" repression.

How, after birth, the maturing organism continues to unfold, by growing planfully and by developing a prescribed sequence of physical, cognitive, and social capacities—all that is described in the literature of child development.

To us, it is first all important to realize that in the sequence of significant experiences the healthy child, if properly guided, can be trusted to conform to the epigenetic laws of development as they now create a succession of potentialities for significant interaction with a growing number of individuals and with the mores that govern them. While such interaction varies widely from culture to culture, all cultures must guarantee some essential "proper rate" and "proper sequence," their propriety corresponding to what Hartmann (1939) referred to as "average expectable"; that is, what is necessary and manageable for all humans, no matter how they differ in personality and cultural pattern.

Epigenesis, then, by no means signifies a mere succession. It also determines certain laws in the fundamental relations of the growing parts to each other—as the diagram below attempts to formalize:

	Part 1	Part 2	Part 3
Stage III	1_{III}	2_{III}	3_{III}
Stage II	1_{II}	2_{II}	3_{II}
Stage I	1_{I}	2_{I}	3_{I}

The heavily lined boxes along the ascending diagonal demonstrate both a sequence of stages (I, II, III) and a development of component parts (1, 2, 3); in other words, the diagram formalizes a *progression through time of a differentiation of parts.* This indicates that *each part* (say, 2_I) *exists* (below the diagonal) in some form *before "its" decisive and critical time normally arrives* (2_{II}) *and remains systematically related to all others* (1 and 3) *so that the whole ensemble depends on the proper development in the proper sequence of each item.* Finally, as each part comes to its full ascendance and finds some lasting solution during its stage (on the diagonal) it will also be expected to develop further (2_{III}) under the dominance of subsequent ascendancies (3_{III}) and most of all, to take its place in the integration of the whole ensemble (1_{III}, 2_{III}, 3_{III}). Let us now see what implications such a schema may have for pregenitality and (later) for psychosocial development.

Pregenitality is so pervasive a concept in psychoanalytic literature that it will suffice to summarize here those of its essential features on which a psychoanalytic theory of development must be based. The child's erotic experiences are called pregenital because sexuality reaches genital primacy only in puberty. In childhood, sexual development undergoes three phases, each of which marks the strong *libidinization* of a vital zone of the organism. Therefore, they are usually referred to as the "oral," the "anal," and the "phallic" phases. The far-reaching consequences of their strong libidinal endowment for the vicissitudes of human sexuality have been abundantly demonstrated—that is, the playful variety of pregenital pleasures (if, indeed, they remain "forepleasures"); the ensuing perversions, if one or the other remains demanding enough to upset the genital primacy; and, above all, the neurotic consequences of the undue repression of strong pregenital needs. Obviously, these three stages, too, are linked epigenetically, for anality (2_I) exists during the oral stage (I) and must take its place in the "phallic" stage (III), after its normative crisis in the anal stage (2_{II}).

Granted all this, the question remains: Does pregenitality, as an intrinsic part of man's prolonged childhood, only exist for and borrow significance from the development of sexuality?

From a psychobiological viewpoint it is most obvious that these "erotogenic" zones and the stages of their libidinization seem central to a number of other developments basic to survival. There is, first of all, the fundamental fact that they serve functions necessary for the preservation of the organism: the intake of food and the elimination of waste—and, after some delay called sexual latency, the procreative acts preserving the species. The sequence of their erotization, furthermore, is intrinsically related to the contemporaneous growth of other organ systems.

Let us consider here in passing one of the functions of the human hand; namely, the mediation between autoerotic experiences and their sublimation. The arms, with all their defensive and aggressive functions, are also "arranged" so that the hands can serve as the sensitive conveyors of manipulatory excitement even as they are the dextrous executors of most complex activities such as are served also by man's special eye-hand coordination. All this is of outstanding importance in the play age, to which we ascribe the psychosocial conflict of *initiative* vs. *guilt*— where guiltiness, of course, rules against habitual autoerotism and the fantasies it serves, while initiative opens manifold avenues of sublimation in dextrous play and in basic patterns of work and communication. To begin with, then, one must throughout relate the erotogenic zones and periods to all the developing sensory, muscular, and locomotor organ systems, and thus speak of:

(1) an *oral-respiratory* and *sensory* stage
(2) an *anal-urethral* and *muscular* stage
(3) an *infantile-genital* and *locomotor* stage

These stages and all their part aspects, in turn, must be visualized in the epigenetic order charted in the small diagram (page 28). At the same time, it may prove helpful to the reader to localize these stages in column A on Chart 1, (pages 32–33) which lists a survey of some of the themes gradually to be related to each other in this essay.

As we now approach the question as to how these organ systems also "acquire" psychosocial significance, we must first of all remember that the stages of prolonged human childhood (with all their instinctual variability) and the structure of human communities (in all their cultural variation) are part of one evolutionary development and must have a built-in potential for serving each other. Communal institutions can, in principle, be expected to support the developmental potentials of the organ systems, even though, at the same time, they will insist on giving each part function (as well as childhood as a whole) specific connotations which may support cultural norms, communal style, and the dominant world view, and yet may also cause unecological conflict.

But as to the specific question of how the community responds to the erotic experience and expression associated with each stage of pregenitality, we face a historical dilemma of interpretation, for the clinical observations of psychoanalysis that led to the discovery of the stages of pregenitality only permitted the conclusion that, by its very nature, "society" as such is so hostile to infantile sexuality that it becomes a matter of more or less strict repression, amounting, at times, to an all-human suppression. Such potential repression, however, can be said to have been uniquely monomanic in the Victorian period of history and specifically pathogenic in creating its prime neuroses; namely, hysteria and compulsion neurosis. And while psychiatry and psychoanalysis can and must always discover such "new" aspects of human nature as are reflected in the epidemiological trends of the times, their interpretation must, at any given time, allow for what we will discuss later as *historical relativity*. Periods not specifically inclined to train children with excessive moralism do permit, up to a point, a direct playing out of infantile sexual trends. And all societies must, in principle, cultivate an instinctually endowed interplay of adults and children by offering spe-

Chart 1

Stages	A Psychosexual Stages and Modes	B Psychosocial Crises	C Radius of Significant Relations
I Infancy	Oral-Respiratory, Sensory- Kinesthetic (Incorporative Modes)	Basic Trust vs. Basic Mistrust	Maternal Person
II Early Childhood	Anal-Urethral, Muscular (Retentive- Eliminative)	Autonomy vs. Shame, Doubt	Parental Persons
III Play Age	Infantile-Genital, Locomotor (Intrusive, Inclu- sive)	Initiative vs. Guilt	Basic Family
IV School Age	"Latency"	Industry vs. Inferiority	"Neighbor- hood," School
V Adoles- cence	Puberty	Identity vs. Identity Con- fusion	Peer Groups and Outgroups; Models of Leadership
VI Young Adulthood	Genitality	Intimacy vs. Isolation	Partners in friendship, sex, competition, cooperation
VII Adulthood	(Procreativity)	Generativity vs. Stagnation	Divided Labor and shared household
VIII Old Age	(Generalization of Sensual Modes)	Integrity vs. Despair	"Mankind" "My Kind"

D Basic Strengths	E Core- pathology Basic Antipathies	F Related Princi- ples of Social Order	G Binding Ritualiza- tions	H Ritualism
Hope	Withdrawal	Cosmic Order	Numinous	Idolism
Will	Compulsion	"Law and Order"	Judicious	Legalism
Purpose	Inhibition	Ideal Proto-types	Dramatic	Moralism
Competence	Inertia	Technological Order	Formal (Technical)	Formalism
Fidelity	repudiation	Ideological Worldview	Ideological	Totalism
Love	Exclusivity	Patterns of Cooperation and Compe-tition	Affiliative	Elitism
Care	Rejectivity	Currents of Education and Tradition	Generational	Authoritism
Wisdom	Disdain	Wisdom	Philosophical	Dogmatism

cial forms of "dialogue" by which the child's early physical experiences are given deep and lasting cultural connotations. As the maternal and the paternal person, and then various parental persons, come within the radius of the child's readiness for instinctual attachment and interplay, the child in turn evokes in these adults corresponding patterns of communication of long-range significance for communal as well as individual integration.

ORGAN MODES AND POSTURAL AND SOCIAL MODALITIES

PREGENITAL MODES

We now nominate for the prime link between psychosexual and psychosocial development the *organ modes* dominating the psychosexual zones of the human organism. These organ modes are *incorporation, retention, elimination, intrusion,* and *inclusion;* and while various apertures can serve a number of modes, the theory of pregenitality maintains that each of the libidinal zones during "its" stage is dominated both pleasurably and purposefully by a primary mode-configuration of functioning. The mouth primarily *incorporates,* even as it can also eject content or close itself up to incoming matter. The anus and the urethra *retain* and *eliminate,* while the phallus is destined to intrude, and the vagina to *include.* But these modes also comprise basic configurations that dominate the interplay of a mammalian organism and its parts with another organism and its parts, as well as with the world of things. The zones and their modes, therefore, are the focus of some prime concerns of any culture's child-training systems, even as they remain, in their further development, central to the culture's "way of life." At the same time, their first experience in childhood is, of course, significantly related to the *postural* changes and modalities that are so basic to an organism destined to be upright—from proneness to crawling; from sitting and standing to walking and running—with all their resulting changes in perspective. These include the proper spatial behavior expected from the two sexes.

On first acquaintance with "primitive" childrearing methods, one cannot help concluding that there is some instinctive wisdom in the way in which they use the instinctual forces of pregenitality not only by making the child sacrifice some strong wishes in a significant way, but also by helping the child to enjoy as well as to perfect adaptive functions from the most minute daily habits to the techniques required by the dominant technology. Our reconstruction of the original Sioux child training made us believe that what we will later describe and discuss as basic trust in early infancy was first established by the almost unrestricted attentiveness and generosity of the nursing mother. While still nursing during the teething stage, she would playfully aggravate the infant boy's ready rage in such a way that the greatest possible degree of latent ferocity was provoked. This was apparently to be channelized later into customary play and then into work, hunting and warring demanding competent aggressiveness against prey and enemy. Thus, we concluded, primitive cultures, beyond giving specific meanings to early bodily and interpersonal experience in order to create the "right" emphases on both organ modes and social modalities, appear to channelize carefully and systematically the energies thus provoked and deflected; and they give consistent supernatural meaning to the infantile anxieties that they have exploited by such provocation.

In elaborating on some of the early social modalities related to organ modes, let me resort to basic English, for its spare verbal usage can best convey for us those behaviors that are fundamental to all languages and invite and permit systematic comparison.

The *oral-sensory stage* is dominated by two modes of incorporation. *To get* means at first to receive and to accept what is given;

and there is, of course, a truly fundamental significance in the similarity between the modes of breathing and those of sucking. The "sucking" mode is the first social modality learned in life, and is learned in relation to the maternal person, the "primal other" of first narcissistic mirroring and of loving attachment. Thus, in *getting what is given*, and in learning to *get somebody to give* what is wished for, the infant also develops the necessary adaptive groundwork to, some day, *get to be* a giver. But then, the teeth develop and with them the pleasure in biting *on* things, in biting *through* them, and in biting bits *off* them. This more active-incorporative mode, however, also characterizes the development of other organs. The eyes, first ready to accept impressions as they come along, are learning to focus, to isolate, and to "grasp" objects from the vaguer background—and to follow them. Similarly, the ears learn to discern significant sounds, to localize them, and to guide a searching turn toward them, even as the arms learn to reach out aimfully and the hands to grasp firmly. All these modalities are given widely different connotations in the context of earlier or later weaning and longer or shorter dependence. We are, then, dealing here not with a simple causal effect of training on development but, as we promised, with *a mutual assimilation of somatic, mental, and social patterns:* an adaptive development that must be guided by a certain inner logic in cultural patterns (a logic later to be discussed as *ethos*) tuned as it must be to the ego's growing capacity to adaptively integrate its "apparatuses."

As to the simple and functional alternative of *holding on* and *letting go*, some cultures—and probably those where possessiveness is central to the cultural ethos—will tend to underscore the *retentive* and *eliminative modes* normatively dominating the anal-muscular stage and may make a battleground of these zones. In their further development, such modes as *to hold* can turn into a destructive and cruel retaining or restraining, or they can support a pattern of care, *to have and to hold*. To *let go*, likewise, can turn into an inimical letting loose of destructive forces, or it can become a relaxed "to let pass" and "to let be." In the meantime, a sense of defeat (from too many conflicting double meanings and too little or too much training) can lead to deep shame and a compulsive doubt whether one will ever be able to feel that one willed what one did—or did what one willed.

The *intrusive* mode, dominating much of the behavior of the third stage, the *infantile-genital*, characterizes a variety of configurationally "similar" activities: the intrusion into space by vigorous locomotion; into other bodies by physical attack; into other people's ears and minds by aggressive sounds; and into the unknown by consuming curiosity. Correspondingly, the *inclusive* mode may express itself in the often surprising alteration of such aggressive behavior with a quiet, if eager, receptivity in regard to imaginative material and a readiness to form tender and protective relations with peers as well as with smaller children. True, the first libidinization of penis and vagina can be manifested in autoerotic play and in oedipal fantasies, although where conditions permit they can also be dramatized in joint sexual play, including a mimicry of adult intercourse. But all this will soon give way to "latency," while the ambulatory and infantile-genital stage adds to the inventory of generalized modalities that lend themselves to basic English that of "making," in the sense of "being on the make." The word suggests *initiative*, insistence on goal, pleasure of conquest. Again, some cultures are apt to cultivate in the boy a greater emphasis on "making" by intrusive modes and in the girl a "making" by teasing and provoking or by other forms of "catching"; that is, by making herself attractive and endearing. And yet, both sexes have a combination of all these modalities at their disposal.

Here, a word should be said concerning the fact that, instead of the original "phallic phase," I prefer to speak of an *infantile-genital* stage, and to consider it dominated in both sexes by combinations of intrusive and inclusive modes and modalities. For at the infantile-genital level—and this seems to be one of the (evolutionary) "reasons" for the latency period—a certain bisexual disposition must be assumed in both sexes, while a full differentiation of the genital modes of male intrusion and female inclusion must wait for puberty. True, the girl's observation of the boy's visible and erectile organ may, especially in patriarchal settings, lead to some penis envy, but it will also and more simply introduce the strong wish to eventually include the penis where it seems to want to visit. The very fact, however, that we are speaking not only of organ modes but also of social modalities of intrusion and inclusion as developmentally essential for both boys and girls demands a shift of theoretical emphasis in regard to female development: (1) from the exclusive sense of loss of an external organ to a budding sense of vital inner potential—the "inner space," then—that is by no means at odds with a full expression of vigorous intrusiveness in locomotion and in general patterns of initiative; and (2) from a "passive" renunciation of male activity to the playful pursuit of activities consonant with and expressive of the possession of birth-giving and nurturant organs. Thus, a certain bisexual propensity for the alternate use of both the intrusive and the inclusive modes allows for greater cultural and personal variation in the display of gender differences, while not foreclosing a full genital differentiation in puberty.

The alternation between the inclusive and intrusive modes does, of course, lead to specific conflicts in male childhood. It is true that at this age of great physical concerns, the observation of the female genitals is apt to arouse in boys a castration fear, which may inhibit identifications with female persons. And yet, when permitted expression under enlightened conditions, such identifications can foster the development in boys of caring qualities not incommensurate with vigorous locomotion and eventually intrusive genitality.

A full consideration of the final fate of the genital zones, modes, and modalities must help to clarify certain universal feminine and masculine problems that may have to be understood in their developmental complexity before the now so obvious traditional exploitability of sexual differences becomes fully understandable. There is an undeniable affinity between inclusive and incorporative modes. In the female, given the absence of a phallic potential for intrusion (and a postponement of breast development), this affinity can aggravate under given cultural conditions a tendency toward taking refuge in dependence. This, in turn, can lead to a collusion with the exploitative trends of some cultures, and especially so in connection with the dependent conditions resulting from exclusive and unlimited procreative responsibilities. At least in some cultural schemes, and together with a radical division of the economic function of the two sexes, this tendency may, in human evolution, have contributed to a certain exploitability of the female as one who expects, as she is expected, to remain dependent even while, or especially when, taking effective care of infantile (and adult) dependents.[2] In the male, on the other hand, any corresponding need for regressive dependence or, in fact, a nurturant identification with the mother could, under the same cultural conditions, well lead to a militant overcompensation in the direction of intrusive pursuits, such as hunting or warring, competing— or exploiting. What becomes, in either sex, of the countermodes, therefore, deserves comparative study, and this most vigilantly at a time when all theoretical conclusions in such matters are drawn into an acute ideological discord. The main point is that the social experiments of today and the available insights must eventually lead to a sexual ethos convincing enough to children of both sexes as well as to liberated adults.

POSTURAL MODALITIES

As we review the fate of the organ modes of the erogenous zones and relate them to the modalities of social existence, it

---

[2] While, in principle, I believe in such an evolutionary potential and the necessity to become aware of it, I must admit that its presentation in a chart of modes and zones (Erikson 1963) can be misleading in its configurational oversimplification.

becomes important to point more systematically to the psychosocial significance of the sensory, muscular, and locomotor modalities during the very period of pregenitality. The child undergoing these states exists, as we have noted in passing, in an *expanding space-time* experience as well as in an expanding *radius of significant social interplay.*

Psychoanalytic theory has not made much of the difference between the changing conditions of being supine or crawling or upright and walking during the stages of psychosexuality, even though the very riddle posed to Oedipus pronounces their fundamental importance: "What walks on four feet in the morning, in midday on two, and on three in the evening?" Let me, then, begin once more with earliest posture and attempt to illustrate the way in which it determines (in consonance with the psychosexual and psychosocial stages) some basic perspectives in space-time existence.

The newborn, recumbent, is gradually looking up and searching the inclined and responsive face of the motherly person. Psychopathology teaches that this developing eye-to-eye relationship (J. Erikson, 1966) is a "dialogue" as essential for the psychic development and, indeed, survival of the whole human being as is the mouth-to-breast one for its sustenance: the most radical inability to "get in touch" with the maternal world first betraying itself in the lack of eye-to-eye encounter. But where such contact is established, the human being will thereafter always look for somebody to look up to and all through life will feel confirmed by "uplifting" encounters. Thus, in the playful, and yet planful, dialogue that negotiates the first interpersonal encounters, the light of the *eyes*, the features of the *face*, and the sound of the *name* become essential ingredients of a first recognition of and by the primal other. Their lasting existential value is attested to by the way in which these ingredients are said to return in decisive encounters throughout life, be it in that of lovers who "drink to me only with thine eyes"; or in that enchantment of the masses, which (as in the Indian "darshan") "drink in" the presence of a charismatic figure; or in the lasting search for a divine countenance—as in St. Paul's promise that we shall penetrate the "glass darkly" and shall "know even as we also are known." Modern accounts of the reported experience of individuals who seem to have returned from a certified death appear to confirm the vision of such an ultimate meeting.

As we enlarge here on the significance of man's initial proneness, we cannot omit mention of the ingenious arrangement of the basic psychoanalytic treatment situation that, paradoxically, permits free association under the condition that the patient maintain a supine position which forbids a meeting of the eyes during a most fateful exchange of words. Such mixture of freedom and constriction, is indeed, bound to lead to passionate and persistent transferences, the most profound (and, to some, disturbing) of which may well be a repetition of the supine infant's (deprived) search for the caretaking person's responsive face.

Human development is dominated by dramatic shifts in emphasis; and while at first confirmed in its singularly long infantile dependence, the human child soon and with a vengeance must learn to "stand on its own (two!) feet," acquiring a firmness of upright position that creates new perspectives with a number of decisive meanings, as homo ludens also becomes homo erectus.

For the creature who stands upright, the (at first a bit wobbly) head is on top, the eyes in front. Our stereoscopic vision thus makes us "face" what is ahead and in front. What is behind is also in back; and there are other significant combinations: ahead and above; ahead and below; behind and above; and behind and below; all of which receive in different languages strong and varied connotations. What is ahead and above can guide me like a light, and what is below and in front can trip me up, like a snake. Who or what is in the back is not visible, although it can see me; wherefore shame is related not only to the consciousness of being exposed in front, when upright, but also of having a back—and especially a "behind." Those who are "behind me" thus fall into such contradictory categories as those who are "backing me up" and guiding me in going ahead; or those who are watching me when I do not know it, and those who are "after me," trying to "get me." Below and behind are those things and people whom I simply may have outgrown, or those that I want to leave behind, forget, discard. Here, the eliminative mode can be seen to assume a generalized ejective modality, and there are, of course, very many other systematic and significant combinations of organ modes and postural perspectives, which I must leave the reader to pursue. In the meantime, the reader may have noticed (as I just did) that in this paragraph I have written in terms of an experiencing "I." And, indeed, every step in development which is receiving experiential and linguistic confirmation also validates not only the (unconscious) ego but also the conscious "I" as the steady center of self-awareness—a combination as central to our psychic life as is our breathing to our somatic existence.

In regard to all of this, the postural (as well as modal) logic of language is one of the prime guarantors to the growing child that "his individual way of mastering experience (his ego synthesis) is a successful variant of a group identity and is in accord with its space-time and life plan." We shall return to this.

A child, finally, who has just achieved the ability to walk seems not only driven to repeat and to perfect the act of walking with a flair of drivenness and an air of mastery, but will also soon be inclined, in line with the intrusiveness of the infantile-genital stage, to a variety of invasions into the sphere of others. Thus, in all cultures, the child becomes aware of the new status and stature of "one who can walk," with all its often contradic-tory connotations: be it "he who will go far," or "he who might go too far," or "she who moves nicely," or "she who might tend to 'run around.' " Thus, walking, as any other developmental achievement, must contribute to a self-esteem that reflects the conviction that one is learning competent steps toward some shared and productive future and acquiring a psychosocial iden-tity on the way.

As to the child's emerging inner structure, which must be related and remain related to the cultural "outerworld," psychoanalysis has emphasized the ways in which, during childhood, the parents' prohibitions and prescriptions are internalized to become part of the *super*ego; that is, an inner, higher-than-thou voice that makes you "mind"; or an ego *ideal* that makes you anxiously or proudly look up to your higher self and helps you later to find and trust mentors and "great" leaders.

RITUALIZATION

What so far has been called rather vaguely a "dialogue" or interplay between the growing child and caring adults takes on more psychosocial presence when we describe one of its most significant characteristics, namely, *ritualization*. This term is taken over from ethology, the study of animal behavior. It was coined by Julian Huxley (1966) for certain phylogenetically performed "ceremonial" acts in the so-called social animals, such as the flamboyant greeting ceremonies of some birds. But here we must take note that the words "ceremonies" and "ceremonial" in this context make sense only in quotation marks—as does the word "ritual," say, when used as a clinical characterization of a hand-washing compulsion. Our term ritualization, luckily, is less pretentious, and in a human context is used only for a certain kind of informal and yet prescribed interplay between persons who repeat it at meaningful intervals and in recurring contexts. While such interplay may not mean much more (at least to the participants) then "this is the way *we* do things," it has, we claim, adaptive value for all participants and for their group living. For it furthers and guides, from the beginning of existence, that stagewise instinctual investment in the social process that must do for human adaptation what the instinctive fit into a section of nature will do for an animal species.

To choose an everyday analogy to the animal ritualizations described so vividly by J. Huxley and K. Lorenz (1966), we call to mind the human mother's approach to greeting her infant on awakening or, indeed, the ways in which the same mother feeds or cleans her infant or puts the infant to sleep. It becomes clear, then, that what we call ritualization in the human context can, at the same time, be highly individual ("typical" for the particular mother and tuned to the particular infant) and yet also, to any outside observer, seem recognizably stereotyped along some traditional lines subject to anthropological comparison. The whole procedure is superimposed on the periodicity of physical and libidinal needs as it responds to the child's growing cognitive capacities and the eagerness to have disparate experiences made coherent by mothering. The mother in her postpartum state is also needful in a complex manner; for whatever instinctual gratification she may seek in being a mother, she also needs to become a mother of a special kind and in a special way. This first human ritualization, then, while fulfilling a series of uses and duties, supports that joint need, already discussed, for a mutuality of recognition, by face and by name. And here, while we are always inclined to pair an infant with its mother, we must of course allow for other maternal persons and, indeed, for fathers, who help to evoke and to strengthen in the infant the sense of a *primal Other*—the I's counterpart.

Wherever and whenever this element is repeated, such meetings at their best reconcile seeming paradoxes: they are playful and yet formalized; they become familiar through repetition and yet seem always surprising. Needless to say, such matters, while they can be as simple as they seem "natural," are not altogether deliberate and (like the best things in life) cannot be contrived. And yet, they serve the permanent establishment of what in daily usage has (unfortunately) come to be called the "object" relationship—unfortunately, because here a term technically meaningful for insiders as part of the libido theory (for the loved person is an "object" of the *libido*) is generalized with possibly "unavowed" consequences (Erikson 1978). The most passionately loved person is called an "object," and this misnomer takes the word *object* away from the world of *factual things:* the world in which the child must also invest uniquely important emotional as well as cognitive interests. At any rate, the psychosexual aspect of the matter is complemented by the psychosocial capacity to confront the existence of a primary Other as well as to comprehend oneself as a separate self—in the light of the other. At the same time, it counteracts the infant's rage and anxiety, which seem to be so much more complex and fateful than the young animal's upsets and fears. Correspondingly, a lack of such early connection can, in extreme cases, reveal an "autism" on the part of the child that corresponds or probably is responded to by some maternal withdrawal. If so, we can sometimes observe a fruitless exchange, a kind of private ritualism characterized by a lack of eye contact and facial responsiveness and, in the child, an endless and hopeless repetition of stereotyped gestures.

I must now admit that one additional justification for applying the terms ritualization and ritualisms to such phenomena is, in fact, a correspondence between everyday ritualizations and the grand rituals of the culture in which they take place. I suggested earlier that the mutual recognition between mother and infant may be a model of some of the most exalted encounters throughout life. This, in fact, may now serve to make it plausible that the ritualizations of each of the major stages of life correspond to one of the major institutions in the structure of societies—and to their rituals. I submit that this first and dimmest affirmation of the described polarity of "I" and "Other" is basic to a human being's ritual and esthetic needs for a pervasive quality which we call the *numinous:* the aura of a hallowed presence. The numinous assures us, ever again, of *separateness transcended* and yet also of *distinctiveness confirmed*, and thus of the very basis of a sense of "I." Religion and art are the institutions with the strongest traditional claim on the cultivation of numinosity, as can be discerned in the details of rituals by which the numinous is shared with a congregation of other "I" 's—all now sharing one all-embracing "I Am (Jehovah)" (Erikson 1981). Monarchies have competed with this claim, and in modern times, of course, political ideologies have taken over the numinous function, with the face of the leader multiplied on a thousand banners. But it is too easy for skeptical observers (including clinicians who, besides a powerful technique, partake in a professional "movement," with a founder's picture on the wall and a heroic prehistory as ideological guide) to consider traditional needs for such inclusive and transcendant experiences a partial regression to what appear to be infantile needs—or forms of mass psychosis. Such needs must be studied in all their developmental and historical relativity.

It is true, however, that every basic ritualization is also related to a form of *ritualism,* as we call ritual-like behavior patterns marked by stereotyped repetition and illusory pretenses that obliterate the integrative value of communal organization. Thus, the need for the numinous under given conditions easily degenerates into *idolatry,* a visual form of addiction that, indeed, can become a most dangerous collective delusional system.

To characterize (more briefly) the primary ritualizations of the second (*anal-muscular*), and third (*infantile genital-locomotor*) stages: In the second stage the question arises as to how the willful pleasure adhering to the functions of the muscular system (including the sphincters) can be guided into behavior patterns fitting the cultural mores, and this by an adult will that must become the child's own will. In the ritualizations of infancy, cautions and avoidances were the parents' responsibility; now the child himself must be trained to "watch himself" in regard to what is possible and/or permissible and what is not. To this end, parents and other elders compare him (to his face) to what he might become if he (and they) did not watch out, thus creating two opposite self-images: one which characterizes a person on the way toward the kind of expansion and self-assertion desired in his home and in his culture; and one (most fateful) negative image of what one is not supposed to be (or show) and yet what one potentially is. These images may be reinforced by unceasing references to the kind of behavior for which the child is as yet too small, or just the right age, or already too big. All this takes place within a radius of significant attachments which now include both older children and parental persons, with the father figure being seen as more and more central. Maybe it is up to the muscular authority figure with the deeper voice to underscore the Yes's and No's and yet to balance the threatening and forbidding aspects of his appearance with a benevolent and guiding guardianship.

Clinically, we know the pathological results of a decisive disturbance at this stage. It is again a failure of the ritualizations that define the small individual's leeway in such a manner that some basic choices remain guaranteed even as certain areas of self-will are surrendered. And so, the ritualized acceptance of the necessity to differentiate between right and wrong, good and bad, mine and thine, may degenerate either into an overly compulsive compliance or, indeed, into a compulsive impulsivity. The elders, in turn, demonstrate their inability to carry through productive ritualization by indulging in compulsive or impulsive, and often most cruel, ritualisms themselves.

This stage is the arena for the establishment of another great principle of ritualization. I call it the *judicious* one, for it combines "the law" and "the word": to become ready to accept the spirit of the word that conveys lawfulness is an important aspect of this development. Here, then, is the ontogenetic origin of that great human preoccupation with questions of free will and of self-determination, as well as of the lawful definition of guilt and transgression. Correspondingly, the institutions rooted in this phase of life are those that define by law the individual's freedom of action. The corresponding rituals are to be found in the judicial system, which makes all-visible on the public stage of the courts a drama that is familiar to each individual's inner life: for the law, we must be made to believe, is untiringly watchful, as is, alas, our conscience; and both must declare us free as they condemn the guilty. Thus, the judicious element is another intrinsic element of man's psychosocial adaptation, as rooted in ontogenetic development. But the danger of ritualism lurks here, too. It is *legalism*, which—now too lenient and now too strict— is the bureaucratic counterpart to individual compulsivity.

The *play age*, finally, is a good stage with which to close the description of the ritualizations of preschool life. Psychosexually speaking, the play age must resolve the oedipal triad governing the basic family, while intensive extrafamilial attachments are postponed to a time after the child has passed the school age, whatever the society's method of first schooling may be. In the meantime, the play age entrusts the vastly increased sphere of initiative to the capacity of children to cultivate their own sphere of ritualization; namely, the world of miniature toys and the shared space-time of games. These are apt to absorb in imaginative interplay both excessive dreams of conquest and the resulting guilt.

The basic element of ritualization contributed by the play age is the infantile form of the *dramatic*. The epigenetic chart, however, will insist that the dramatic does not replace but rather joins the numinous and the judicial elements, even as it anticipates the elements as yet to be traced ontogenetically; namely, the *formal* and the *ideological*. No adult ritual, rite, or ceremony can dispense with any of these. The institutions corresponding to the child's play sphere, however, are the stage-or-screen, which specializes in the awe-filled or humorous expression of the dramatic, or other circumscribed arenas (the forum, the temple, the court, the common) in which dramatic events are displayed. As for the element of ritualism rooted in the play age, I think it is a moralistic and inhibitive suppression of playful initiative in the absence of creatively ritualized ways of channeling guilt. *Moralism* is the word for it.

Having arrived at the connection between play and drama it seems appropriate to say a word about the psychosocial significance of the infantile fate of King Oedipus who was, of course, the hero of a play. In charting some aspects of the organismic order, we have so far neglected the increasing number of *counter-*

players with whom the growing child (via the zones, the modes, and the modalities) can enter into meaningful interplay. First there is, of course, the maternal person who in the stage of symbiosis permits the libido to be attached to the *primal other*[3] who, as we saw, also becomes the guarantor of a kind of self-love (for which Narcissus seems, indeed, to be a somewhat special case) and thus provides that *basic trust* which we will presently discuss as the most fundamental syntonic attitude.

It is when this original *dyad* develops into a *triad* including the father(s) that the "conflictuous" conditions for the Oedipus complex are given; that is, a strong instinctual wish to possess the parent of the other sex forever and the consequent jealous hate of the (also loved) parent of the same sex. The psychosexual aspects of this early attachment have made up the very *core complex* of psychoanalysis. Here we must add, however, that these passionate wishes are carefully scheduled to be at their height when the somatic chances for their consumption are totally lacking while playful imagination is flourishing. Thus prime instinctual wishes as well as the corresponding reactions of guilt are scheduled to appear at a period of development that combines the most intense infantile conflict with the greatest advance in playfulness, while whatever fantastic wishes—and guilt feelings—come to flourish are scheduled to be submerged in the next "latency" and school stage. With the advent, in turn, of genital maturation in adolescence and its eventual direction toward sexual mates, the remnants of infantile fantasies of oedipal conquest and competition are linked with those of age mates who share idealized heroes and leaders (governing concrete areas and arenas as well as "theaters" and worlds). All these are endowed with instinctual energies on which the social order must count for its generational renewal.

In passing, however, we must note another essential attribute

[3] The term, "other," is taken from Freud's letters to Fliess, where Freud confesses to seek "the Other" ("*der Andere*") in his correspondent (Freud 1887–1902). (See also Erikson 1955).

of all developmental unfolding. As the radius of counterplayers increases, graduating the growing being into ever new roles within wider group formations, certain basic configurations such as the original dyad or triad demand to find a new representation within later contexts. This does not give us the right, without very special proof, to consider such reincarnations as a mere sign of fixation or regression to the earliest symbiosis. They may well be instead an epigenetic recapitulation on a higher developmental level and, possibly, attuned to *that* level's governing principles and psychosocial needs. A charismatic or divine image, in the context of the ideological search of adolescence or the generative communality of adulthood, is not "nothing but" a reminder of the first "Other." As Blos (1967) has called it, there can be "regression in the service of development."

I conclude this chapter on the generational implications of epigenetic development with some summary remarks on play. The original play theory of psychoanalysis was, in accord with its energy concepts, the "cathartic" theory, according to which play had the function in childhood of working off pent-up emotions and finding imaginary relief for past frustrations. Another plausible explanation was that the child utilized the increasing mastery over toys for playful arrangements that permitted the illusion of also mastering some pressing life predicaments. For Freud, play, above all, turned enforced passivity into imaginary activity. In accord with the developmental viewpoint, I at one time postulated an *autosphere* for play with the sensations of the body; a *microsphere* for toys; and a *macrosphere* for play with others. Of great help in clinical play was the observation that the microsphere of toys can seduce the child into an unguarded expression of dangerous wishes and themes that then arouse anxiety and lead to—most revealing—sudden *play disruption*, the counterpart in waking life of the anxiety dream. And indeed, if thus frightened or disappointed in the microsphere, the child may regress into the autosphere, daydreaming, thumbsucking, masturbating. Developmentally, however, playfulness reaches into the macrosphere, that is the social arena shared with others, where it must be learned which playful intentions can be shared with others—and forced upon them. Here, soon, the great human invention of formal games, combining aggressive aims with rules of fairness, takes over. Play, then, is a good example of the way in which every major trend of epigenetic development continues to expand and develop throughout life. For the ritualizing power of play is the infantile form of the human ability to deal with experience by creating model situations and to master reality by experiment and planning. It is in crucial phases of his work that the adult, too, "plays" with past experience and anticipated tasks, beginning with that activity in the autosphere called thinking. But beyond this, in constructing model situations not only in open dramatizations (as in "plays" and in fiction) but also in the laboratory and on the drawing board, we inventively anticipate the future from the vantage point of a corrected and shared past as we redeem our failures and strengthen our hopes. In doing so, we obviously must learn to accept and make do with those materials—be they toys or thought patterns, natural materials or invented techniques—that are put at our disposal by the cultural, scientific, and technological conditions of our moment of history.

And so, epigenesis strongly suggests that we do not make play and work mutually exclusive. There is an early form of serious work in the earliest play, while some mature element of play does not hinder, but augments true seriousness in work. But then, adults have the power to use playfulness and planfulness for most destructive purposes; play can become a gamble on a gigantic scale, and to play one's own game can mean to play havoc with that of others.

All the themes of the Play Age, however—of initiative inhibited by guilt; of fantasies materialized in toy things; of play space psychosocially shared; and of the saga of Oedipus—all these themes remind us of that other, that most private stage-and-screen: the dream. From its verbalization and analysis we have learned immeasurably, and yet we must bypass it in this psycho-social account: except to point out that the dream, so far studied primarily in regard to its "latent" hidden content, can be very instructive in its "manifest" use of modes and modalities (Erikson 1977).

Having now sketched the succession up through childhood, of such basic elements of psychosocial development as modes and modalities, ritualization and play, I must return once more to the psychosexual theory, which ascribes such specific contributions of instinctual energy to the child's pregenital development.

The theory of psychosexuality depicts as the goal of pregenital development the mutuality of genital potency of the two sexes. It makes much of adult maturation, and most of adult freedom from neurosis, dependent on this accomplishment. Whatever this libido "is," however, its transformations into psychosocial development could, as we have seen, not be effected without the adults' devoted, and at times passionate or driven, interaction with the generational challenge. Therefore, the logic of a truly complete psychosexual theory may well demand that some instinctual drive toward procreation and a generative interplay with offspring be assumed to exist in human nature as a counterpart to the adult animal's instinctive involvement in the creation and care of offspring (Benedek 1959). Thus, as we complete column A of Chart 1, we add (in parenthesis) a *procreative* stage that represents the instinctual aspect of the psychosocial stage of *generativity* (column B).

When I postulated this in an address presented to the International Psychoanalytic Congress in New York in 1979 (Erikson 1980c), I illustrated the universality of the theme by pointing out that in the classical form of *Oedipus Rex*, the king is by no means accused only of a genital crime. Oedipus is said throughout to have "ploughed the field where he himself was sown" (Knox 1957); and as a result, all the land had turned barren and the women infertile.

However, to underline the procreative aspect of psychosexuality may, I admitted, appear highly paradoxical (if not unethical) at a time when birth control must become universal. Still, it is and will be the task of psychoanalysis to point to the possible dangers of radical changes in psychosexual ecology (as was, in fact, its original mission in the Victorian age), so that their effects may be recognized in clinical work—and beyond. And it could well be, for example, that some exaggerated concern with the "Self," as observed in today's patients, may be ascribed in some to a repression of the wish for procreation and the denial of the resulting sense of loss. But there is, of course, always an alternative to pathogenic suppression, namely, *sublimation;* that is, the use of libidinal forces in psychosocial contexts. Consider only the increased capacity of some contemporary adults to "care" for children not "biologically" their own, whether in their homes, their schools, or, indeed, in "developing" parts of the world. And *generativity* always invites the possibility of an energetic shift to *productivity* and *creativity* in the service of the generations.

3

Major Stages in Psychosocial Development

ABOUT THE TERMS USED—AND THE CHARTS

To RESTATE the sequence of psychosocial stages throughout life means to take responsibility for the terms Joan Erikson and I have originally attached to them—terms that include such suspect words as *hope*, *fidelity*, and *care*. These, we say, are among the psychosocial strengths that emerge from the struggles of syntonic and dystonic tendencies at three crucial stages of life: hope from the antithesis of *basic trust* vs. *basic mistrust* in infancy; fidelity from that of *identity* vs. *identity confusion* in adolescence; and care from *generativity* vs. *self absorption* in adulthood. (The *vs.* stands for "versus," and yet also, in the light of their complementarity, for something like "vice versa.") Most of these terms seem not foreign to the claim that, in the long run, they represent basic qualities that, in fact, "qualify" a young person to enter the generational cycle—and an adult to conclude it.

In regard to our terms in general, I will quote the late theoretical arbiter, David Rapaport. Having tried to assign to me a firm

Chart 2

Psychosocial Crises

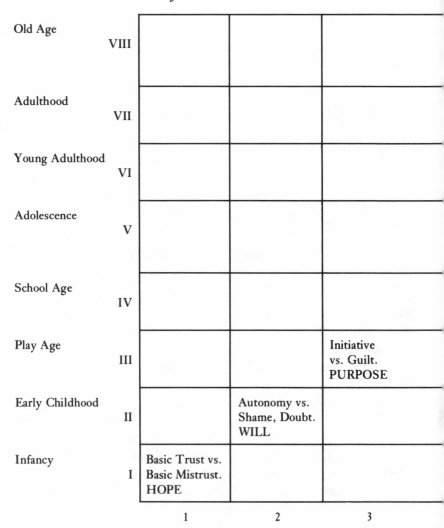

		1	2	3
Old Age	VIII			
Adulthood	VII			
Young Adulthood	VI			
Adolescence	V			
School Age	IV			
Play Age	III			Initiative vs. Guilt. PURPOSE
Early Childhood	II		Autonomy vs. Shame, Doubt. WILL	
Infancy	I	Basic Trust vs. Basic Mistrust. HOPE		

				Integrity vs. Despair, disgust. WISDOM
			Generativity vs. Stagnation. CARE	
		Intimacy vs. Isolation. LOVE		
	Identity vs. Identity Confusion. FIDELITY			
Industry vs. Inferiority. COMPETENCE				

| 4 | 5 | 6 | 7 | 8 |

place in ego psychology, he cautioned his readers: "Erikson's theory (like most of Freud's) ranges over phenomenological, specifically clinical psychoanalytic-psychological propositions, without systematically differentiating among them. Correspondingly, the conceptual status of this theory's terms is so far unclear" (Rapaport in Erikson 1959). The readers of this tract will know what he is talking about. But if we accept the proposition that ritualization is one link between developing egos and the ethos of their communality, living languages must be considered one of the most outstanding forms of ritualization in that they express both what is universally human and what is culturally specific in the values conveyed by ritualized interplay. Thus, when we approach the phenomena of human strength, the everyday words of living languages, ripened in the usage of generations, will serve best as a basis of discourse.

More specifically, if developmental considerations lead us to speak of *hope*, *fidelity*, and *care* as the human strengths or ego qualities emerging from such strategic stages as infancy, adolescence, and adulthood, it should not surprise us (though it did when we became aware of it) that they correspond to such major credal values as *hope*, *faith*, and *charity*. Skeptical Vienna-trained readers, of course, will be reminded of the Austrian emperor who, when asked to inspect the model of a new flamboyant baroque memorial, declared with authority, "You need a bit more faith, hope, and charity in the lower left corner!" Such proven traditional values, while referring to the highest spiritual aspirations, must, in fact, have harbored from their dim beginnings some relation to the developmental rudiments of human strength; and it would be most instructive to pursue such parallels in different traditions and languages.

For my talk on the generational cycle, in fact, I asked Sudhir Kakar for the Hindu term corresponding to Care. He answered that there did not seem to be one word for it, but that the adult is said to fulfill his tasks by practicing *Dáma* (Restraint), *Dāna* (Charity), and *Daya* (Compassion). These three words, I could only reply, are well translated into everyday English with "to be care-ful," "to take care of," and "to care for" (Erikson 1980). But here, it may be helpful to call to mind the sequence of these stages on the developmental ladder suggested by the epigenetic viewpoint, as indicated in Chart 2. Especially since I intend, instead of always "to begin again with the beginning," to start this discussion of the psychosocial stages high up on the last level of adulthood, it seems important to take a quick and reassuring look at the whole ladder leading up to it. To complete the list of strengths, it will be seen that between those of hope and fidelity we postulate (in firm relation to the major developmental rungs) the steps of *will, purpose,* and *competence,* and between fidelity and care, a step of *love.* Beyond care, we even claim something called *wisdom.* But the chart also makes clear in its verticals that each step (even wisdom) is grounded in all the previous ones; while in each horizontal, the developmental maturation (and psychosocial crisis) of one of these virtues gives new connotations to all the "lower" and already developed stages as well as to the higher and still developing ones. This can never be said often enough.

On the other hand, one may well ask how it is that we find the *epigenetic* principle so practical in depicting the overall configuration of *psychosocial* phenomena; does this not mean to give a somatic process exclusive organizing power over a social one? The answer must be that the stages of life remain throughout "linked" to somatic processes, even as they remain dependent on the psychic processes of personality development and on the ethical power of the social process.

The epigenetic nature of this ladder, then, can be expected to be reflected in a certain linguistic coherence of all terms. And indeed, such words as *hope, fidelity,* and *care* have an inner logic that seems to confirm developmental meanings. *Hope* is "expectant desire," a phrase well in accordance with a vague instinctual drivenness undergoing experiences that awaken some firm expectations. It is also well in accord with our assumption that this first basic strength and root of ego development emerges from the resolution of the first developmental antithesis; namely, that of *basic trust* vs. *basic mistrust*. And as to suggestive linguistic connotations, hope seems to be related even to "hop" which means to leap; and we have always made the most of the fact that Plato thought the model of all playfulness to be the leap of young animals. At any rate, hope bestows on the anticipated future a sense of leeway inviting expectant leaps, either in preparatory imagination or in small initiating actions. And such daring must count on basic trust in the sense of a trustfulness that must be, literally and figuratively, nourished by maternal care and—when endangered by all-too-desperate discomfort—must be restored by competent consolation, the German *Trost*. Correspondingly, *care* reveals itself as the instinctual impulse to "cherish" and to "caress" that which in its helplessness emits signals of despair. And if, in adolescence, the age mediating between childhood and adulthood, we postulate the emergence of the strength of *fidelity* (fidé-lité, fedeltà), this is not only a renewal on a higher level of the capacity to trust (and to trust oneself), but also the claim to be trustworthy, and to be able to commit one's loyalty (the German *Treue*) to a cause of whatever ideological denomination. A lack of confirmed fidelity, however, will result in such pervasive symptomatic attitudes as diffidence or defiance, and even a faithful attachment to diffident or defiant cliques and causes. Thus, trust and fidelity are linguistically as well as epigenetically related, and we see in our sickest young individuals, in adolescence, semideliberate regression to the earliest developmental stage in order to regain—unless they lose it altogether—some fundamentals of early Hope from which to leap forward again.

To point to a developmental logic in such universal values as faith, hope, and charity, however, does not mean to reduce them, in turn, to their infantile roots. Rather, it forces us to consider how emerging human strengths, step for step, are intrinsically beset not only with severe vulnerabilities that perpetually demand our healing insights, but also with basic evils which call for the redeeming values of universal belief systems or ideologies. So, somewhat encouraged, we will present the psychosocial stages. And, as I said, I will this time begin with the last stage—that is, the top line of our chart—and this not only out of methodological contrariness, but in order to further the logic of the chart. As stated, the reading of the chart demands that any line—horizontal or vertical—must be developmentally related to any other, whether in the form of an earlier condition or of a later consequence of demonstrable necessity. And this, it would seem, must be possible to carry through in the case of a stage which acutely demands new attention and concern in our day.

THE LAST STAGE

The dominant antithesis in old age and the theme of the last crisis we termed *integrity* vs. *despair.* Here, the dystonic element may seem more immediately convincing, considering the fact that the top line marks the total end (unpredictable in time and kind) of this, our one given course of life. Integrity, however, seems to convey a peculiar demand—as does the specific strength that we postulate as maturing from this last antithesis—namely, *wisdom.* This we have described as a kind of "informed and detached concern with life itself in the face of death itself," as expressed in age-old adages and yet also potentially present in the simplest references to concrete and daily matters. But then again, a more or less open *disdain* is the antipathic counterpart to wisdom—a reaction to feeling (and seeing others) in an increasing state of being finished, confused, helpless.

Before we try to make sense of such terminal contradictions we may well ponder again the historical relativity of all development and, especially also, of all developmental theories. Take this last stage: It was in our "middle years" that we formulated it—at a time when we certainly had no intention of (or capacity for) imagining ourselves as really old. This was only a few decades ago; and yet, the predominant image of old age was then altogether different. One could still think in terms of "elders," the few wise men and women who quietly lived up to their stage-appropriate assignment and knew how to die with some dignity in cultures where long survival appeared to be a divine gift to and a special obligation for a few. But do such terms still hold when old age is represented by a quite numerous, fast-increasing, and reasonably well-preserved group of mere "elderlies"? On the other hand, should historical changes dissuade us from what we have once perceived old age to be, in our own lifetime and according to the distilled knowledge that has survived in folk wit as well as in folk wisdom?

No doubt, the role of old age needs to be reobserved, rethought. To this we can here try to contribute only by reviewing our scheme. So back to the chart: What is the place of old age in the length and the width of it? Located as it is chronologically in the upper right corner, its last dystonic item, we said, is *despair*; and as we take a quick glance at the lower left corner we remember that down there the first syntonic element is *hope*. In Spanish, at least, this bridges *esperanza* and *desesperanza*. And indeed, in whatever language, hope connotes the most basic quality of "I"-ness, without which life could not begin or meaningfully end. And as we ascend to the empty square in the upper left corner, we realize that up there we need a word for the last possible form of hope as matured along the whole first ascending vertical: for this, certainly, the word *faith* suggests itself.

If, then, at the end the life cycle turns back on the beginnings, there has remained something in the anatomy even of mature hope, and in a variety of faiths ("Unless you turn and become like children . . ."), which confirms hopefulness as the most childlike of all human qualities. And indeed, the last stage of life seems to have great potential significance for the first; children in viable cultures are made thoughtful in a specific way by encounters with old people; and we may well ponder what will and must become of this relationship in the future when a ripe old age will be an "averagely expectable" experience, to be planfully anticipated. Thus, a historical change like the lengthening of the average life span calls for viable reritualizations, which must provide a meaningful interplay between beginning and end as well as some finite sense of summary and, possibly, a more active anticipation of dying. For all this, *wisdom* will still be a valid word—and so, we think, will *despair*.

Returning once more to the upper right corner, we retrace one step back along the diagonal only to reenter the *generative* stage that preceded old age. But in an epigenetic scheme, we said, "after" should mean only a later version of a previous item, not a loss of it. And indeed, old people can and need to maintain a *grand*-generative function. For there can be little doubt that today the discontinuity of family life as a result of dis-location contributes greatly to the lack in old age of that minimum of vital involvement that is necessary for staying really alive. And lack of vital involvement often seems to be the nostalgic theme hidden in the overt symptoms that bring old people to psychotherapy. Much of their despair is, in fact, a continuing sense of stagnation. This, it is said, may make some old people try to prolong their therapies (King 1980), a new symptom easily mistaken for a mere regression to early stages: and this, especially when old patients seem to be mourning not only for time forfeited and space depleted but also (to follow the top line of our chart from left to right) for autonomy weakened, initiative lost, intimacy missed, generativity neglected—not to speak of identity potentials bypassed or, indeed, an all too limiting identity lived. All of this, as we said, may be "regression in the service of development" (Blos 1967)—that is, a search for the solution of a (literally) *age-specific conflict.*

We will return to these questions in the final chapter. Here we wish to emphasize in passing that in old age all qualities of the past assume new values that we may well study in their own right and not just in their antecedents—be they healthy or pathological. In more existential terms, that the last stage finds one relatively freer of neurotic *anxiety* does not mean one is absolved from the *dread* of life-and-death; the most acute understanding of infantile *guilt* does not do away with the sense of *evil* that in each life is experienced in its own way, just as the best-defined psychosocial *identity* does not preempt the existential "I." In sum, a better-functioning ego does not synthesize away the aware "I." And the social ethos must not abrogate its responsibility for these ultimate perspectives that in history have been prophetically envisaged by religious and political ideologies.

But to complete the review of our psychosocial conclusions: If the antipathic counterpart of wisdom is disdain, this (like all antipathies), must up to a point be recognized as a natural and necessary reaction to human weakness and to the deadly repetitiveness of depravity and deceit. Disdain, in fact, is altogether denied only at the danger of indirect destructiveness and more or less hidden self-disdain.

What is the last ritualization built into the style of old age? I think it is *philo-sophical:* for in maintaining some order and meaning in the dis-integration of body and mind, it can also advocate a durable hope in wisdom. The corresponding ritualistic danger, however, is *dogmatism*, a compulsive pseudointegrity that, where linked to undue power, can become coercive orthodoxy.

And what final psychosexual state can we suggest for (pre-senile) old age? I think it is a *generalization of sensual modes* that can foster an enriched bodily and mental experience even as part functions weaken and genital energy diminishes. (Obviously, such extensions of the libido theory call for discussion and are therefore rendered in parenthesis on Chart 1.)

And so we return to what we claimed to be the dominant syntonic trait in the last stage; namely, *integrity*. This in its simplest meaning is, of course, a sense of *coherence* and *wholeness* that is, no doubt, at supreme risk under such terminal conditions as include a *loss of linkages* in all three organizing processes: in the Soma, the pervasive weakening of tonic interplay in connecting tissues, blood-distributing vessels, and the muscle system; in the Psyche, the gradual loss of mnemonic coherence in experience, past and present; and in the Ethos, the threat of a sudden and nearly total loss of responsible function in generative interplay. What is demanded here could be simply called "integrality," a tendency to keep things together. And indeed, we must acknowledge in old age a retrospective mythologizing that can amount to a pseudointegration as a defence against lurking despair. (Such defensive use can, of course, be made of all syntonic qualities dominating the chart's diagonal.) Yet throughout, we must allow for a human being's potential capacity, under favorable conditions, more or less actively to let the integrative experience of earlier stages come to fruition; and so, our chart allows, up the rightmost vertical, for the gradual maturation of integrity.

So let me take another look at the way we put all this when we first formulated integrity: But if the old in some respects become again like children, the question is whether this "turn" is to a childlikeness seasoned with wisdom or to a finite childishness. (The old may become, or want to become, too old too fast or remain too young too long.) Here, only some sense of integrity can bind things together; and by integrity we cannot mean only a rare quality of personal character but above all a shared proclivity for understanding or for "hearing" those who do understand, the integrative ways of human life. It is a comradeship with the ordering ways of distant times and different pursuits, as expressed in their simple products and sayings. But there emerges also a different, a timeless love for those few "Others" who have become the main counterplayers in life's most significant contexts. For individual life is the coincidence of but one life cycle with but one segment of history; and all human integrity stands or falls with the one style of integrity of which one partakes.

THE GENERATIONAL LINK: ADULTHOOD

Having now reviewed the end of the life cycle as much as my context permitted, I do feel an urgency to enlarge on a "real" stage—that is, one that mediates between *two* stages of life—and of the generational cycle itself. This sense of urgency seems best expressed in the story of the old man who was dying. As he lay there with his eyes closed, his wife whispered to him, naming every member of the family who was there to wish him shalom. "And *who*," he suddenly asked, sitting up abruptly, "*who is minding the store?*" This expresses the spirit of adulthood which the Hindus call "the maintenance of the world."

Our two adult stages, *adulthood* and *young adulthood*, are not meant to preempt all the possible substages of the period between adolescence and old age; yet, appreciative as we are of the alternative subdivisions suggested by other workers, we repeat our original conclusions here—primarily in order to convey the global logic of any such scheme. This means, within the re-view attempted here, that as we proceed to the next preceding stage it should above all prove to have been developmentally indispensable for the later stages already described. As to the age range appropriate to all such stages, it stands to reason that they are circumscribed by the earliest moment at which, considering all the necessary conditions, a developmental quality *can* come to relative dominance and to a meaningful crisis, and the latest moment at which, for the sake of overall development, it *must* yield that critical dominance to the next quality. In this succession, rather wide temporal ranges are possible; but the *sequence* of stages remains predetermined.

To adulthood (our seventh stage) we have assigned the critical antithesis of *generativity* vs. *self-absorption and stagnation.* Generativity, we said, encompasses *procreativity, productivity,* and *creativity,* and thus the generation of new beings as well as of new products and new ideas, including a kind of self-generation concerned with further identity development. A sense of stagnation, in turn, is by no means foreign even to those who are most intensely productive and creative, while it can totally overwhelm those who find themselves inactivated in generative matters. The new "virtue" emerging from this antithesis, namely, Care, is a widening commitment to *take care of* the persons, the products, and the ideas one has learned *to care for.* All the strengths arising from earlier developments in the ascending order from infancy to young adulthood (hope and will, purpose and skill, fidelity and love) now prove, on closer study, to be essential for the generational task of cultivating strength in the next generation. For this is, indeed, the "store" of human life.

Is not procreativity, then (we have asked), a further step rather than a mere byproduct of genitality (1980(c))? Since every genital encounter engages the procreative organs in some arousal and in principle can result in conception, a psychobiological need for procreation can, it seems, not be ignored. At any rate, the young adults' capacity (acquired in the preceding stage of *intimacy* vs. *isolation*) to lose themselves so as to find one another in the meeting of bodies and minds, is apt to lead sooner or later to a vigorous expansion of mutual interests and to a libidinal investment in that which is being generated and cared for together. Where generative enrichment in its various forms fails altogether, regressions to earlier stages may occur either in the form of an obsessive need for pseudo-intimacy or of a compulsive kind of preoccupation with self-imagery—and both with a pervading sense of stagnation.

Stagnation, like the antitheses in all stages, marks the potential core pathology of this stage and will, of course, involve some regression to previous conflicts. Yet it must be understood also in its stage-specific importance. This, as indicated, is especially important today when *sexual frustration* is recognized as pathogenic, while *generative frustration*, according to the dominant technological ethos of birth control, is apt to remain unrecognized. Yet, sublimation, or a wider application, is the best use of frustrated drive energies. Thus today, as we have said, a new generative ethos may call for a more *universal care* concerned with a qualitative improvement in the lives of all children. Such new caritas would make the developed populations offer the developing ones, beyond contraceptives and food packages, some joint guarantee of a chance for the vital development as well as for the survival—of every child born.

But here I must continue the account of those other sets of phenomena characteristic of every stage of life that are of fateful consequence for group life and for the survival of mankind itself. If care (as all other strengths cited) is the expression of a vital *sympathic* trend with a high instinctual energy at its disposal, there is also a corresponding *antipathic* trend. In old age, we called such a trend disdain; in the stage of generativity, it is *rejectivity*; that is, the unwilligness to include specified persons or groups in one's generative concern—one *does not care to care* for them. There is, of course, a certain logic to the fact that in man the (instinctual) elaboration of (instinctive) caretaking tends to be highly selective in favor of what is or can be made to be most "familiar." In fact, one cannot ever be generative and care-ful without being selective to the point of *some* distinct rejectivity. It is for this very reason that ethics, law, and insight must define the bearable measure of rejectivity in any given group, even as religious and ideological belief systems must continue to advocate a more universal principle of care for specified wider units of communities. It is here, in fact, where such spiritual concepts as a universal caritas give their ultimate support to an extending application of developmentally given care. And caritas has much to keep in abeyance, for rejectivity can express itself in intrafamilial and communal life as a more or less well-rationalized and more or less ruthless suppression of what does not seem to fit some set goals of survival and perfection. This can mean physical or moral cruelty against one's children, and it can turn, as moralistic prejudice, against other segments of family or community. And, of course, it can lump together as "the other side" large groups of foreign peoples. (At any rate, it is a task of every case study to make explicit the way in which some of our young patients are types who have become the focus of the rejectivity of generations—and not merely of a "rejecting mother.")

Rejectivity, furthermore, periodically finds a vast area for collective manifestation—such as in wars against (often neighboring) collectivities who once more appear to be a threat to one's own kind, and this not only by dint of conflicting territorialities or markets, but simply by seeming dangerously different—and who, of course are apt to reciprocate this sentiment. The conflict between generativity and rejection, thus, is the strongest ontogenetic anchor of the universal human propensity that I have called *pseudospeciation*. Konrad Lorenz fittingly translates it as *Quasi-Artenbildung* (1973); that is, the conviction (and the impulses and actions based on it) that another type or group of persons are, by nature, history, or divine will, a species different from one's own—and dangerous to mankind itself.[4] It is a prime human dilemma that pseudospeciation can bring out the truest and best in loyalty and heroism, cooperation and inventiveness, while committing different human kinds to a history of reciprocal enmity and destruction. The problem of human rejectivity, then,

[4] The word "pseudo," in its naturalist meaning, does not imply deliberate deception. Rather, it suggests a grandiose, all-human tendency to create more or less playfully appearances that make one's own kind a spectacular and unique sight in creation and in history—a potentially creative tendency, then, that can lead to most dangerous extremes.

has far-reaching implications for the survival of the species as well as for every individual's psychosocial development; where rejectivity is merely inhibited, there may well be self-rejection.

In accordance with our promise, we must also allocate to each stage a specific form of *ritualization*. An adult must be ready to become a numinous model in the next generation's eyes and to act as a judge of evil and a transmitter of ideal values. Therefore, adults must and do also ritualize being ritualizers; and there is an ancient need and custom to participate in some rituals that ceremonially sanction and reinforce that role. This whole adult element in ritualization we may simply call the *generative* one. It includes such auxiliary ritualizations as the parental and the didactic, the productive and the curative.

The *ritualism* potentially rampant in adulthood is, I think, *authoritism*—the ungenerous and ungenerative use of sheer power for the regimentation of economic and familial life. Genuine generativity, of course, includes a measure of *true authority*.

Mature adulthood, however, emerges from young adulthood, which, psychosexually speaking, depends on a postadolescent genital mutuality as a libidinal model of true intimacy. An immense power of verification pervades this meeting of bodies and temperaments after the hazardously long human preadulthood.

Young adults emerging from the adolescent search for a sense of identity can be eager and willing to fuse their identities in mutual intimacy and to share them with individuals who, in work, sexuality, and friendship promise to prove complementary. One can often be "in love" or engage in intimacies, but the intimacy now at stake is the capacity to commit oneself to concrete affiliations which may call for significant sacrifices and compromises.

The psychosocial antithesis to *intimacy*, however, is *isolation*, a fear of remaining separate and "unrecognized"—which provides a deep motivation for the entranced ritualization of a, now genitally mature, "I"-"you" experience such as marked the beginning of one's existence. A sense of isolation, then, is the potential core pathology of early adulthood. There are, in fact, affiliations that amount to an *isolation à deux*, protecting both partners from the necessity to face the next critical development—that of generativity. But the greatest danger of isolation is a regressive and hostile reliving of the identity conflict and, in the case of a readiness for regression, a fixation on the earliest conflict with the primal Other. This can emerge as "borderline" pathology. From the resolution of the antithesis between intimacy and isolation, however, emerges *love*, that mutuality of mature devotion that promises to resolve the antagonisms inherent in divided function.

The antipathic counterforce to young adult intimacy and love is *exclusivity*, which, in form and function, is of course closely related to the *rejectivity* emerging in later adulthood. Again, some exclusivity is as essential to intimacy as rejectivity is to generativity; yet both can become vastly destructive—and self-destructive. For the incapacity to reject or exclude anything at all can only lead to (or be the result of) excessive self-rejection and, as it were, self-exclusion.

Intimacy and generativity are obviously closely related, but intimacy must first provide an *affiliative* kind of ritualization that cultivates styles of ingroup living held together by often extremely idiosyncratic ways of behaving and speaking. For intimacy remains the guardian of that elusive and yet all-pervasive power in psychosocial evolution, the power of communal and personal *style:* which gives and demands conviction in the shared patterns of living; guarantees some individual identity even in joint intimacy; and binds into a way of life the *solidarity* of a joint commitment to a *style of production*. These, at least, are the high goals to which development, in principle, is tuned. But then, this is the stage when persons of very different backgrounds must fuse their habitual ways to form a new milieu for themselves and their offspring: a milieu reflecting the (gradual or radical) change of mores and the shifts in dominant identity patterns being brought about by historical change.

The ritualism apt to make an unproductive caricature of the ritualizations of young adulthood is *elitism*, which cultivates all sorts of cliques and clans marked more by snobbery than by a living style.

ADOLESCENCE AND SCHOOL AGE

To proceed further back: the reliability of young adult commitments largely depends on the outcome of the adolescent struggle for identity. Epigenetically speaking, of course, nobody can quite "know" who he or she "is" until promising partners in work and love have been encountered and tested. Yet, the basic patterns of identity must emerge from (!) the selective affirmation and repudiation of an individual's childhood identifications; and (2) the way in which the social process of the times identifies young individuals—at best recognizing them as persons who had to become the way they are and who, being the way they are, can be trusted. The community, in turn, feels recognized by the individual who cares to ask for such recognition. By the same token, however, society can feel deeply and vengefully rejected by the individual who does not seem to care to be acceptable, in which case society thoughtlessly dooms many whose ill-fated search for communality (in gang loyalty, for example) it cannot fathom or absorb.

The antithesis of identity is *identity confusion*, obviously a normative and necessary experience that can, however, form a core disturbance aggravating and aggravated by pathological regression.

How is the psychosocial concept of identity related to the

self—that core concept of individual psychology? As pointed out, a pervasive sense of identity brings into gradual accord the variety of changing self-images that have been experienced during childhood (and that, during adolescence, can be dramatically recapitulated) and the role opportunities offering themselves to young persons for selection and commitment. On the other hand, a lasting sense of self cannot exist without a continuous experience of a conscious "I," which is the numinous center of existence: a kind of *existential identity*, then, which (as we noted in discussing old age) in the "last line" must gradually transcend the psychosocial one. Therefore, adolescence harbors some sensitive, if fleeting, sense of existence as well as a sometimes passionate interest in ideological values of all kinds—religious, political, intellectual—including, at times, an ideology of adjustment to the time's patterns of adjustment and success. Here, the upheavals characterizing the adolescence of other times can remain strangely dormant. And then again, adolescence can harbor existential preoccupations of the kind that can "come of age" only in old age.

The specific strength emerging in adolescence—namely, *fidelity*—maintains a strong relation both to infantile trust and to mature faith. As it transfers the need for guidance from parental figures to mentors and leaders, fidelity eagerly accepts their ideological mediatorship—whether the ideology is one implicit in a "way of life" or a militantly explicit one. The antipathic counterpart of fidelity, however, is *role repudiation:* an active and selective drive separating roles and values that seem workable in identity formation from what must be resisted or fought as alien to the self. Role repudiation can appear in the form of *diffidence* covering a certain slowness and weakness in relation to any available identity potential or in the form of a systematic *defiance*. This last, is a perverse preference for the (always also present) *negative identity;* that is, a combination of socially unacceptable and yet stubbornly affirmed identity elements. If the social setting fails to offer any viable alternatives, all this can lead to a sudden and sometimes "borderline" regression to the conflicts of the earliest experiences of the sense of "I," almost as a desperate attempt at self-rebirth.

Yet again, an identity formation is impossible without *some* role repudiation, especially where the available roles endanger the young individual's potential identity synthesis. Role repudiation, then, helps to delimit one's identity and invokes at least experimental loyalties that can then be "confirmed" and transformed into lasting affiliations by the proper ritualizations or rituals. Nor is some role repudiation expendable in the societal process, for continued readaptation to changing circumstances can often only be maintained with the help of loyal rebels who refuse to "adjust" to "conditions" and who cultivate an indignation in the service of a *renewed wholeness* of ritualization, without which psychosocial evolution would be doomed.

In summary, the process of identity formation emerges as an *evolving configuration*—a configuration that gradually integrates constitutional givens, idiosyncratic libidinal needs, favored capacities, significant identifications, effective defenses, successful sublimations, and consistent roles. All these, however, can only emerge from a mutual adaptation of individual potentials, technological world views, and religious or political ideologies.

The spontaneous ritualizations of this stage can, of course, appear surprising, confusing, and aggravating in the shiftiness of the adolescents' first attempts to ritualize their interplay with age mates and to create small group rituals. But they also foster participation in public events on sports fields and concert grounds and in political and religious arenas. In all of these, young people can be seen to seek a form of ideological confirmation, and here spontaneous rites and formal rituals merge. Such search, however, can also lead to fanatic participation in militant ritualisms marked by *totalism;* that is, a totalization of the world image so illusory that it lacks the power of self-renewal and can become destructively fanatic.

Adolescence and the ever more protracted apprenticeship of

the later school and college years can, as we saw, be viewed as a psychosocial *moratorium:* a period of sexual and cognitive maturation and yet a sanctioned postponement of definitive commitment. It provides a relative leeway for role experimentation, including that with sex roles, all significant for the adaptive self-renewal of society. The earlier school age, in turn, is a *psychosexual moratorium,* for its beginning coincides with what psychoanalysis calls the "latency" period, marked by some dormancy of infantile sexuality and a postponement of genital maturity. Thus the future mate and parent may first undergo whatever method of schooling is provided for in his society and learn the technical and social rudiments of a work situation. We have ascribed to this period the psychosocial crsis of *industry* vs. *inferiority*—the first being a basic sense of competent activity adapted both to the laws of the tool world and to the rules of cooperation in planned and scheduled procedures. And again, one can say that a child at this stage learns to love to learn as well as to play—and to learn most eagerly those techniques which are in line with the *ethos of production.* A certain hierarchy of *work roles* has already entered the playing and learning child's imagination by way of ideal examples, real or mythical, that now present themselves in the persons of instructing adults, and in the heroes of legend, history, and fiction.

For the antithesis of a sense of industry we have postulated a sense of *inferiority*, again a necessary dystonic sense, that helps drive on the best even as it can (temporarily) paralyze the poorer workers. As core *pathology* of this stage, however, inferiority is apt to encompass much fateful conflict; it can drive the child to excessive competition or induce it to regress—which can only mean a renewal of infantile-genital and oedipal conflict, and thus a preoccupation in fantasy with conflictual personages rather than an actual encounter with the helpful ones right at hand. The rudimentary strength developing at this stage, however, is *competence*, a sense that in the growing human being must gradually integrate all the maturing methods of verifying and mastering *factuality* and of sharing the *actuality* of those who cooperate in the same productive situation.

We have now attempted to point up the nexus of instinctual forces and organismic modes within a context of the sequence of psychosocial stages and the succession of generations. We emphasized primarily some principles of development, the inter-disciplinary recognition of which seemed essential at the time of their formulations, although we cannot insist on the exact number of stages listed or, indeed, on all the terms used; clearly, for any overall confirmation of our scheme we remain dependent on a number of disciplines which in these pages were bypassed.

On the psychological side, there is the verifying power of *cognitive growth* as it refines and expands with each stage the capacity for accurate and conceptual interplay with the factual world. This certainly is a most indispensable "ego-apparatus" in Hartmann's sense (1939). So it may prove useful to trace the relation of the "sensory-motor" aspects of intelligence in Piaget's sense to infantile trust; of the "intuitive-symbolic" ones to play and initiative; of "concrete-operational" performance to the sense of industry; and finally, of "formal operations" and "logical manipulations" to identity development (see Greenspan 1979). Piaget, who patiently listened at some of our early interdisciplinary meetings to what is outlined here, later confirmed that he saw at least no contradiction between his stages and ours. "Piaget," Greenspan reports, "is quite sympathetic to Erikson's extension of Freudian theory into psychosocial modes" (1979). And he quotes him: "The great merit of Erikson's stages . . . is precisely that he attempted, by situating the Freudian mechanisms within more general types of conduct (walking, exploring, etc.) to postulate continual integration of previous acquisitions at subsequent levels' " (Piaget 1960).

The antipathic counterpart of *industry*, the sense of competent mastery to be experienced in the school age, is that *inertia* that constantly threatens to paralyze an individual's productive life and is, of course, fatefully related to the *inhibition* of the preceding age, that of *play*.

THE PRESCHOOL YEARS

The childhood stages were already discussed in connection with epigenesis, pregenitality, and ritualization. Here, it remains for us to add only a summary statement on their antitheses and antipathies.

Let us return, then, to the play age, in which the antithesis of initiative and guilt comes to its crisis. As we can only repeat, playfulness is an essential ingredient in all the stages to come. But just when oedipal implications force a strong limitation of initiative on the child's relation with parental figures, maturing play liberates the small individual for a dramatization in the microsphere of a vast number of imagined identifications and activities. The play age, furthermore, "occurs" before the limiting advent of the school age, with its defined work roles, and of adolescence, with its experimentation in identity potentials. It is no accident, then, that to this stage is ascribed the infantile origin of the Oedipus drama, which in its mythology, and especially in its perfection as a play on the stage, proves to be a prime example of the lifelong power of human playfulness in all the arts. In playfulness is grounded, also, all sense of humor, man's specific gift to laugh at himself as well as at others.

All this, however, also makes it plausible that in the play age *inhibition* is the antipathic counterpart of initiative—a necessary counterpart in so playful and imaginative a creature. Yet inhibition also proves to be the core pathology in later psychoneurotic disturbances (from the hysterias on) that are rooted in the conflicted oedipal stage.

The stage preceding the play age is that "anal" stage of conflict which was first found to be the infantile "fixation" point in compulsion-neurotic disturbances. Psychosocially speaking, we consider it to be the crisis of *autonomy* vs. *shame* and *doubt*, from the resolution of which emerges rudimentary *will*. As we again look at the place of this stage between the preceding and the succeeding stages, it seems developmentally "reasonable" that what we have just described as initiative could not have developed without a decisive leap from oral sensory dependence to some anal-muscular self-will and to a certain assured self-control. We have indicated earlier how children can alternate between willful impulsivity and slavish compulsiveness; the child will try at times to act totally independent by altogether identifying with his rebellious impulses or to become dependent once more by making the will of others his own compulsion. In balancing these two tendencies, rudimentary will power supports a maturation both of free choice and of self-restraint. The human being must try early to will what can be, to renounce (as not worth willing) what cannot be, and to believe he willed what is inevitable by necessity and law. At any rate, in accord with the double (retentive and eliminative) modes dominating this age, *compulsion* and *impulsivity* are the antipathic counterparts of *will* and, when aggravated and interlocked, can paralyze it.

Even in descending order, it must have become reasonably clear now that what thus grows in steps is indeed an epigenetic ensemble in which no stage and no strength must have missed its early rudiments, its "natural" crisis, and its potential renewal in all later stages. Thus, hope in infancy can already have an element of willfulness that cannot, however, stand being challenged as yet in the way it must be when the crisis of will arrives in early childhood. On the other hand, one glance back at the "last line" makes it appear probable that an infant's hope already has some ingredient that will gradually grow to become faith—although that will be harder to defend against all but the most fanatic devotees of infancy. On the other hand, does not Laotse's name mean "old child" and refer to a newborn with a tiny white beard?

Hope, we have said, emerges from the conflict of basic trust vs. basic mistrust. Hope is, so to speak, pure future; and where mistrust prevails early, anticipation, as we know, wanes both cognitively and emotionally. But where hope prevails, it has, as we indicated, the function of carrying out the numinous image of the primal other through the various forms it may take in the intermediate stages, all the way to the confrontation with the ultimate other—in whatever exalted form—and a dim promise of regaining, forever, a paradise almost forfeited. By the same token, autonomy and will, as well as industry and purpose, are oriented toward a future that will remain open, in play and in preparatory work, for the choices of one's economic, cultural, and historical era. Identity and fidelity, in turn, must begin to commit themselves to choices involving some finite combinations of activities and values. Youth, in alliance with available ideologies, can envisage a wide spectrum of possibilities of "salvation" and "damnation"; while the love of young adulthood is inspired by dreams of what one may be able to do and to take care of together. With the love and care of adulthood, however, there gradually arises a most critical midlife factor, namely, the evidence of a narrowing of choices by conditions already irreversibly chosen—by fate or by oneself. Now conditions, circumstances, and associations have become one's once-in-one-lifetime reality. Adult care thus must concentrate jointly on the means of taking lifelong care of what one has irrevocably chosen, or, indeed, has been forced to choose by fate, so as to care for it within the technological demands of the historical moment.

Gradually, then, and with every new strength, a new time sense appears along with a sense of irrevocable identity: gradually becoming what one has caused to be, one eventually will be what one has been. Lifton (1970) has vastly clarified what it means to be a survivor, but a person in adulthood must also realize (as

Laius did) that a generator will be survived by what he generated. Not that any of this is all too conscious; on the contrary, it seems that the stage of generativity, as long as a threatening sense of stagnation is kept at bay, is pervasively characterized by a supremely sanctioned disregard of death. Youth, in its own way, is more aware of death than adulthood is; although adults, busy as they are with "maintaining the world," participate in the grand rituals of religion, art, and politics, all of which mythologize and ceremonialize death, giving it ritual meaning and thus an intensely social presence. Youth and old age, then, are the times that dream of rebirth, while adulthood is too busy taking care of actual births and is rewarded for it with a unique sense of boisterous and timeless historical reality—a sense which can seem somewhat unreal to the young and to the old, for it denies the shadow of nonbeing.

The reader may now wish to review the categories listed on Chart 1. For each psychosocial stage, "located" as it is between a *psychosexual* one (A) and an expanding *social radius* (C) we list a *core crisis* (B) during which the development of a specific *syntonic* potential (from basic trust [I] to integrity [VIII]) must outbalance that of its *dystonic* antithesis (from *basic mistrust* to senile *despair*). The resolution of each crisis results in the emergence of a *basic strength* or *ego quality* (from *hope* to *wisdom*) (D). But such sympathic strength, too, has an antipathic counterpart (from *withdrawal* to *disdain*) (E). Both syntonic and dystonic and both sympathic and antipathic potentials are necessary for human adaptation because the human being does not share the animal's fate of developing according to an *instinctive* adaptation to a circumscribed natural environment that permits a clear-cut and inborn division of positive and negative reactions. Rather, the human being must be guided during a long childhood to develop *instinctual* reaction patterns of love and aggression that can be mustered for a variety of cultural environments vastly different in technology, style, and world view, although each supporting what Hartmann (1939) has called certain "average expectable" conditions. But where the dystonic and antipathic trends outweigh the syntonic and sympathic, a specific core pathology develops (from psychotic withdrawal to senile depression).

Ego synthesis and communal ethos together tend to support a certain measure of syntonic and sympathic trends, while they attempt to accommodate some dystonic and antipathic ones in the great variability of human dynamics. But these dystonic and antipathic trends remain a constant threat to the individual and social order, wherefore, in the course of history, inclusive belief systems (religions, ideologies, cosmic theories) have attempted to universalize the sympathic human trends by making them applicable to a widening combination of worthy "insiders." Such belief systems, in turn, become an essential part of each individual's development in that their ethos (which "actuates manners and customs, moral attitudes and ideals") is conveyed in daily life through age-specific and stage-adequate *ritualizations* (G). These enlist the energy of growth in the renewal of certain all-embracing principles (from the *numinous* to the *philosophical*). Wherever *ego* and *ethos* lose their viable interconnection, however, these ritualizations threaten to disintegrate into deadening *ritualisms* (from *idolism* to *dogmatism*) (H). Because of their joint developmental roots, there is a dynamic affinity between individual core disturbances and social ritualisms (cf. E and H).

Thus, each new human being receives and internalizes the logic and the strength of the principles of social order (from the cosmic through the legal and the technological to the ideological and beyond) (F) and develops the readiness under favorable conditions to convey them to the next generations. All this, at any rate, must be recognized as one of the essential built-in potentials for development and recovery, even if daily clinical experience and general observation are apt to confront us with the symptoms of unresolved crises in individuals and with the social pathology of ritualistic decomposition.

All of this brings us to the borders of another complementary study here neglected: which would include *the institutional structures and mechanisms* that make for the politics of communality. True, we have attempted to account for the ritualizations of everyday life that provide the link between individual development and social structure: their "politics" is easily discernible in any record or case study of intimate social interplay. And we have, in passing, related the special strengths emerging from trust and hope with religion, from autonomy and will with the law, from initiative and purpose with the arts, from industry and competence with technology and from identity and fidelity with the ideological order. Yet, we must depend on social science for accounts of how, in given systems and periods, leading individuals as well as elites and power groups strive to preserve, to renew, or replace the all-encompassing ethos in productive and political life, and how they tend to support the generative potentials in adults and the readiness for growth and development in those growing up. In my work, I have only been able to suggest an approach to the lives, and to the critical stages within these lives, of two religious-political leaders—namely, Martin Luther and Mohandas Gandhi (1958; 1969)—who were able to translate their personal conflicts into methods of spiritual and political renewal in the lives of a large contingent of their contemporaries.

This leads us to psychohistorical work. But in the conclusion of this essay it seems best in a few brief notes to ask in what way the psychoanalytic method may gain from psychosocial insight and yield observations conducive to it. This brings us back to the very beginning of this review.

4

Ego and Ethos: Concluding Notes

EGO DEFENSE AND SOCIAL ADAPTATION

In *The Ego and the Mechanisms of Defense*, Anna Freud "deals exclusively with one particular problem; that is, with the ways and means by which the ego wards off unpleasure and anxiety, and exercises control over impulsive behavior, affects, and instinctive urges" (1936, p. 5). Thus, the various omnipresent defenses such as *repression* and *regression*, *denial* and *reaction formation*, are treated exclusively as phenomena of *inner economy*. In February 1973, in Philadelphia, on the occasion of a panel devoted to a review of Anna Freud's book (then in its thirty-seventh year), the opportunity offered itself to discuss some of the social and communal implications of the mechanisms of defense. Can *defense mechanisms*, we asked, be shared and thus assume an *ecological value* in the lives of interrelated persons and in communal life?

There are passages in Anna Freud's book that clearly point to such a potential. Most obvious, of course, is the similarity of certain individual defense mechanisms and the grand ritual defenses of communities. Take, for example, the "identification with the aggressor:" There is the little girl who—for whatever acute reasons—is afraid of ghosts and bans them by making peculiar gestures, thus pretending to be the ghost she might meet in the hall. And we may think of "children's games in which through the metamorphosis of the subject into a dreaded object anxiety is converted into pleasurable security" (A. Freud 1936). Correspondingly, there are, throughout cultural history, all the "primitive methods of exorcising spirits" by impersonating them in their most aggressive forms.

Anna Freud reports on some observations in a particular school that in pursuit of modernity had reritualized (as we would say) its procedures, putting "less emphasis on class teaching" and more on "self-chosen individual work" (1936, p. 95). Immediately, some new and yet well-circumscribed defensive behavior of an intimidated and inhibited sort appeared in a number of children previously known to be quite able and popular; their very adaptiveness seemed endangered by the changed demands. A. Freud suggests that such a shared defense, though engaged in genuinely by each individual, could quickly disappear again if the school abandoned its wayward ritualizations. But what are the social mechanisms of such shared defense that in the long run, at any rate, might become habitual and thus permanently change some personalities and careers, as well as the ethos of group life?

Finally, we may well ponder again the social implications of such an adolescent defense mechanism as *intellectualization* in puberty—that is, the seemingly excessive preoccupation with *ideas* including (in the Vienna of that day) "the demand for revolution in the outside world." Anna Freud interprets this as a defense on the part of these youths against "the perception of the new institutional demands of their own id."; that is, the inner, instinctual revolution. This, no doubt, is the *psychosexual* aspect of the matter; but it stands to reason that intellectual defenses appear and are shared in puberty both as a result of the *cognitive gains* of this stage and as an adaptive use of the ritualizations of an *intellectual ethos* characteristic of some times. The societal process, in fact, must count on and acknowledge such adolescent processes, including their periodical excesses, for its readaptation to a changing ethos.

It appears probable, then, that defense mechanisms are not only molded to the individual's instinctual urges that they are to contain but, where they work relatively well, are shared or counterpointed as part of the ritualized interplay of individuals and families as well as of larger units. But where they are weak, rigid, and altogether isolating, defense mechanisms may well be comparable to *individualized* and *internalized ritualisms*.

Anna Freud recalled some of her own experiences as a teacher as well as "long discussions at her clinic as to whether obsessional children of obsessional parents used obsessional mechanisms out of imitation or identification or whether they shared with their parents the danger arising from strong sadistic tendencies and, independently of their parents, used the appropriate defense mechanism" (Journal of the Philadelphia Assn. for Psychoanalysis, 1974).

I AND WE

The discussion of ego-defences brought us back to the period of what at times was called an Ego-Psychology, even as today we are faced with a Self-Psychology with similar aspirations. I myself could not relate either of these directions with psychosocial theory without, paradoxically, discussing what is most individual in man and yet also most basic for a communal sense of "we." I mean the sense of "I" that is the individual's central awareness of being a sensory and thinking creature endowed with language, who can confront a self (composed, in fact, of a number of selves), and can construct a concept of an unconscious ego. I would assume, in fact, that the ego's synthesizing methods in establishing workable defenses against undesirable impulses and affects restore to what we call a sense of "I" certain basic modes of existence now to be discussed—namely, a sense of being *centered* and *active*, *whole* and *aware*—and thus overcome a feeling of being peripheral or inactivated, fragmented, and obscured.

But here we face a strange blind spot in intellectual interest. The "I," an overweening existential, personological, and linguistic fact, is hard to find in dictionaries and in psychological texts. But most important for us, in the psychoanalytic literature Freud's original use of its German equivalent, *Ich*, is habitually translated into "ego" (Erikson 1981). And yet this *ich* is at times most clearly meant to mean "I." This is particularly true where Freud (1923) ascribes to the *Ich* an *"immediacy"* and *"certainty" of experience "on which all consciousness depends"* (italics mine). This is by no means a matter of simple double meaning, but one of decisive conceptual import. For the unconscious can become known only to an immediate and certain consciousness—a consciousness, furthermore, that through evolution and history seems to have reached a decisive state when it must confront itself with rational methods, thus becoming aware of its own denial of the unconscious and learning to study the consequences. Nevertheless, this elemental consciousness, to Freud, seems to have been one of those primal human facts which he took for granted (*selbstverständlich*) and on which, for the moment, he imperiously refused to reflect. Considering the width and the passion of his own aesthetic, moral, and scientific awareness, one must consider this exclusive concentration on the unconscious and on the id an almost ascetic commitment to the study of what is most obscure and yet also most elemental in human motivation. Yet, it should be noted that his method, in order to make the unconscious yield anything, had to employ playfully configurational means such as "free" association, dream, or play itself—all special means of awareness. Systematic interpretation, meanwhile, works toward an expansion of consciousness. And indeed, in a significant passage Freud refers to consciousness as *"die Leuchte,"* which can only be translated as "the shining light" (S. Freud 1933). Typically, he accompanies this almost religious expression with an ironic note and says about consciousness: "As may be said of our life, it is not worth much, but it is all we have. Without the illumination thrown by the quality of consciousness we should be lost in the obscurity of depth psychology." Yet, typically, to his translator the word "illumination" sufficed for *die Leuchte*.

In subjecting the psychoanalytic technique itself to the stringent and ascetic rules that deprive it of the character of a social encounter, Freud put the self-observing "I" and the shared "we" into the exclusive service of the study of the unconscious. This has proven to be a meditative procedure which can yield unheard-of healing insight for those individuals who feel disturbed enough to need it, curious enough to want it, and healthy enough to "take" it—a selection that can make the psychoanalyzed in some communities feel, indeed, like a new kind of elite. But a more systematic study of "I" and "we" would seem to be not only necessary for an understanding of psychosocial phenomena, but also elemental for a truly comprehensive psychoanalytic psychology. I am, of course, aware of the linguistic difficulty of speaking of *the* "I" as we do of *the* ego or *the* self; and yet, it does take a sense of "I" to be aware of a "myself" or, indeed, of a series of myselves, while all the variations of self-experience have in common (and a saving grace it is) the conscious continuity of the "I" that experienced and can become aware of them all. Thus, the "I," after all, is the ground for the simple verbal assurance that each person is a center of awareness in a universe of communicable experience, a center so numinous that it amounts to a sense of being alive and, more, of being the vital condition of existence. At the same time, only two or more persons who share a corresponding world image and can bridge their languages may merge their "I"s into a "we." It could, of course, be of great significance to sketch the developmental context in which the pronouns—from "I" to "we" to "they"—take on their full meaning in relation to the organ modes, the postural and sensory modalities, and the space-time characteristics of world views.

As to the "we," Freud went so far as to assert that "there is no doubt that the tie which united each individual with Christ is also the cause of the tie which unites them with one another" (1921), but then, as we saw, he did so in a discourse on what he called "artificial" groups such as churches or armies. The fact is, however, that all identifications amounting to brotherhoods and sisterhoods depend on a joint identification with charismatic figures, from parents to founders to gods. Wherefore the God above the Sinai, when asked by Moses who he should tell the people had talked to him, introduced himself as "I AM that I AM" and suggested that the people be told "I AM has sent me unto you." This existential meaning is, no doubt, central to the evolutionary step of monotheism and extends to associated patriarchal and monarchic phenomena (Erikson 1981).

Here we are again reminded of the lifelong power of the first mutual recognition of the newborn and the *primal* (maternal) *other* and its eventual transfer to the *ultimate other* who will "lift up His countenance upon you and give you peace." From here we could once more follow the stages of development and study the way in which in given languages the fatherhoods and motherhoods, the sisterhoods and brotherhoods of the "we" come to share a joined identity experienced as most real. But here also it is necessary to amend the very concept of a reality which, as I complained at the beginning, is all too often seen as an "outerworld" to be adjusted to.

THREEFOLD REALITY

The ego as concept and term was not, of course, invented by Freud. In scholasticism it stood for the *unity* of body and soul, and in philosophy in general for the *permanency* of conscious experience. William James (1920) in his letters refers not only to an "enveloping ego to make continuous the times and spaces," but also speaks of *"the ego's active tension,"* a term that connotes the very essence of subjective health. Here, it seems, James (who knew German intimately) thought of the subjective sense of "I" as well as the unconscious workings of a built-in "ego." But it is apparently one of the functions of the ego's unconscious work to integrate experience in such a way that the I is assured a certain centrality in the dimensions of being: so that, (as suggested), it can feel the flux of events like an effective *doer* rather than an impotent sufferer. *Active* and *originating* rather than inactivated (a word to be preferred to "passive," for one can, as it were, be active in a passive manner); *centered* and *inclusive* rather than shunted to the periphery; *selective* rather than overwhelmed; *aware* rather than confounded: all of this amounts to a sense of being *at home* in one's time and place, and, somehow, of feeling *chosen* even as one chooses.

So far, so good. But, as we noticed, when we follow human development through the stages of life, the human problem is such that so basic a sense of centrality depends for its renewal from stage to stage on an increasing number of others: some of them close enough to be individually acknowledged as an "other" in some important segment of life, but for the most part a vague number of interrelated others who seek to confirm their sense of reality by sharing, if not imposing it on ours, even as they also try to delimit theirs against ours. It is for psychosocial reasons, then, that it is not enough to speak of the ego's adjustment to an outer reality. For, conflictual as all human adaptation is, by the time the ego can be said to guide adaptation, it has already absorbed adaptive experiences and introjected intense identifications. In fact, Freud's German model for *reality*, the word *Wirklichkeit* (related as it is to what "works") has pervasively active and interactive connotations and should usually be translated as *actuality* and, I think, understood to mean "mutual activation."

Reality, then, must be said to have a number of indispensable components. They are all dependent, in a psychoanalytic context, on an *instinctuality* wherein, in contrast to the animal's instinctivity, the affective energies are put at the ego's disposal during development and now work for the immersion of maturing capacities in the phenomenal and communal world. Thus, the child can be said to learn to "love" even facts that can be named, verified, and shared, and that, in turn, inform such love.

As to the three indispensable components of a maturing sense of reality, *factuality* is the most commonly emphasized in the usual sense of the "thing" world of facts—to be perceived with a minimum of distortion or denial and a maximum of the validation possible at a given stage of cognitive development and at a given state of technology and science.

A second connotation of the word *reality* is a convincing coherence and order that lifts the known facts into a context apt to make us (more or less surprisingly) realize their nature: a truth value that can be shared by all those who partake of a joint language and world image. "Comprehensibility" (*Begreiflichkeit*, as used by Einstein) would seem to be a fitting word for this aspect of reality.[5] An alternative term is the more visual *contextuality*, for it is the astounding interwovenness of the facts that gives them a certain revelatory significance. And only by maintaining a meaningful correspondence between such threefold reality and the main developmental stages can the communal ethos secure for itself a maximum of energy from a sufficient number of participants.

Reality as a viable world view, then (even if it is modestly called a "Way of Life") is at its best an all-inclusive conception that focuses disciplined attention on a selection of certifiable facts; liberates a coherent vision enhancing a sense of cont⟨

---

[5] Einstein once said that to "comprehend a bodily object" means to attribut⟨ tence" to it. And he adds "the fact that the world of sense experiences is con⟨ is a miracle" (1954).

and actualizes an ethical fellowship with strong work commitments.

World images, finally, must grow with each individual, even as they must be renewed in each generation. We could now review our chapters, from organ modes to postural and sensory modalities, and from the normative crises of life to the antitheses of psychosocial development, and attempt to indicate how world images tend to provide a universal context and meaning for all such experiences. Only thus can the individual "I," as it grows out of the earliest bodily experiences—and out of that early instinctual development that we call narcissistic—learn to have and to share a modicum of a sense of orientation in the universe. Any study of world images, then, must begin with every "I's" needs for a basic space-time orientation and proceed to the community's ways of providing a network of corresponding perspectives, such as the course of the day and the cycle of the year, the division of work and the sharing of ritual events—up to the limits and "boundaries," in K. Erikson's sense (1966), where *outerness* and *otherness* begin.

While I myself have been able to circumscribe such matters only in an unsystematic manner (1974; 1977) as I was trying to sketch perspectives of growing up in the American way of life, I am convinced that clinical psychoanalytic observation can contribute essential insights into the deep unconscious and preconscious involvement of each individual in established and changing world images. For in all their built-in conflicts and destructive antitheses we can study the potential complementarity of somatic, social, and ego organization. Such study, in different historical settings, will be all the more fruitful as psychoanalysis becomes more aware of its own history and its ideological and ethical implications. But only a new kind of cultural history can show how all the details of individual development dovetail with or come to diverge from the grand schemes suggested in the existential cycles of religious belief systems, in the historical postulates of political and economic ideologies, and in the experiential implications of scientific theories.

ETHOS AND ETHICS

The most comprehensive statement in early psychoanalysis on the dynamic relation of ego and ethos is probably a passage in Freud's *New Introductory Lectures on Psycho-Analysis:*

> As a rule, parents and authorities analogous to them follow the precepts of their own super-egos in educating children. . . . Thus a child's super-ego is in fact constructed on the model not of its parents but of its parents' super-ego; the contents which fill it are the same and it becomes the vehicle of tradition and of all the time-resisting judgments of value which have propagated themselves in this manner from generation to generation (1933).

Here, as we see, Freud locates some aspects of the historical process itself in the individual's superego—that inner agency that exerts such moralistic pressure on our inner life that the ego must defend itself against it in order to be relatively free from paralyzing *inner suppression.* Freud then spars briefly with the "materialistic views of history" that, he says, emphasize *political suppression* by claiming that "human 'ideologies' are nothing other than the product and superstructure of their contemporary economic conditions":

> That is true, but very probably not the whole truth. Mankind never lives entirely in the present. The past, the tradition of the race and of the people, lives on in the ideologies of the super-ego, and yields only slowly to the influences of the present and to new changes; and so long as it operates through the super-ego it plays a powerful part in human life, independently of economic conditions (Freud 1933, p. 67).

This statement has far-reaching implications for the psychological study of revolutionary forces and methods; but most astonishingly it seems to suggest that in reconstructing inner-personal dynamics the psychoanalyst could and should note also the superego's function as a vehicle of tradition, and this especially in regard to its resistance to change and liberation—a suggestion that opens major historical trends as reflected in inner conflicts to direct psychoanalytic study. From a developmental point of view, however, I would like to emphasize that what we detect in the superego as remnants of the childhood years is, as Freud suggests, not only the reflection of living ideologies, but also of old ones that have already become moralisms. For the superego, a balancing of the imaginative oedipal stage and the infantile crisis of *initiative* vs. *guilt* is apt to emphasize, above all, a network of *prohibitions* that must fence in an all too playful initiative and help to establish a basic moral or even moralistic orientation.

As I have indicated, I would then consider adolescence the life stage wide open both cognitively and emotionally for new ideological imageries apt to marshal the fantasies and energies of the new generation. Depending on the historical moment, this will alternately confirm or protest the existing order or promise a future one, more radical or more traditional, and thus help to overcome identity confusion. Beyond this, however, we may allocate to *adulthood*—exactly insofar as it has outgrown its excess of infantile moralism or of adolescent ideologism—the potentiality of an *ethical sense* consonant with the generative engagements of that stage and with the necessity for a modicum of mature and far-reaching planning in accord with historical reality. And here even revolutionary leaders must develop and practice their ideologies both with a firm moral sense—and with ethical concern. (As to our developmental insights, generative ethics would suggest some such new version of the Golden Rule as: Do to another what will advance the other's growth even as it advances your own. [Erikson 1964]).

Here, and in passing, it may be good to remember that in outlining the life stages just reserved for the *ritualizations* of man's moral, ideological, and ethical potentials—namely, childhood, adolescence, and adulthood—we warned of the corresponding dangers of three ritualisms: moralism, totalism, and authoritism. Also, it may be good once more to recall the obligation to visualize all developmental and generational factors *epigenetically*—to wit:

	1	2	3
III			ethical
II		ideological	
I	moral		

Thus, there are potentials for ethical and ideological traits in all morality, even as there are both moral and ethical traits in ideology. Therefore, continuing moral or ideological modes of thought in the ethical position are by no means "infantile" or "juvenile" leftovers, as long as they retain the potential for becoming integrated parts of a certain generative maturity within the historical relativity of the times.

HISTORICAL RELATIVITY IN THE PSYCHOANALYTIC METHOD

As we in conclusion return once more to the basic psychoanalytic method, we must remember its two inaleinable functions: it is a Hippocratic undertaking that aims at freeing adults (whether patients or candidates for training) from the oppressive and repressive anxieties of childhood and from their influence on life and personality as already lived; and at the same time it is a didactic as well as a research method that uniquely reveals some of man's fixations on past developments in phylogeny as well as in ontogeny. In this connection it is interesting to note that a striving for an all-human adulthood was part of last century's ethos. Thus, in his 1844 manuscripts Karl Marx claims that "just as all things natural must *become*, man, too, has his act of becoming—history" (Tucker 1961). For "the act of becoming," Marx also uses the word *Entstehungsakt*, which connotes a combination of an active "emerging," "standing up," and "becoming"; and there is the clear implication of the coming maturity of the species. In a comparable utopian statement, Freud said, "I may now add that civilization is a process in the service of Eros, whose purpose is to combine single human individuals, and after that families, then races, peoples, and nations, into one great unity, the unity of mankind" (1930). The implication that such a future demands an all-human adulthood seems to pervade Freud's systematic preoccupation with man's potentially fatal regressive tendencies toward infantile as well as primitive and archaic affects and images; the human being of the future, enlightened about all these "prehistorical" fixations, will perhaps have a somewhat better chance to act as an adult *and* as a knowing participant in one human specieshood. In our terms, this would imply that an adult mankind would overcome pseudo- (or quasi-) speciation; that is, the splitting into imaginary species that has provided adult rejectivity with a most moralistic rationalization of the hate of otherness. Such "speciation" has supported the most cruel and reactionary attributes of the superego where it was used to reinforce the narrowest tribal consciousness, caste exclusiveness, and nationalistic and racist identity, all of which must be recognized as endangering the very existence of the species in a nuclear age.

The word *Eros* in this context once more underscores the fact that a psychoanalytic theory begins with the assumption of all-embracing instinctual forces that, at their best, contribute to a universal kind of love. But it also once more underlines the fact that we have entirely neglected that other unifying life principle, *logos*, that masters the cognitive structure of factuality—a theme of such ever-increasing importance today, when technology and science suggest, for the first time in human history, some outlines of a truly universal and jointly planned physical environment. However, the world suggested in the imagery of universal technology and apt to be dramatized by the media can turn into a vision of a totally fabricated order to be planned according to strictly logical and technological principles—a vision dangerously oblivious of what we are emphasizing in these pages; namely, the dystonic and antipathic trends endangering the organismic existence and the communal order on which the ecology of psychic life depends. An art-and-science of the human mind, however, must be informed by a developmental, or shall we say life-historical, orientation, as well as by a special historical self-awareness. As the historian Collingwood (1956) puts it: "History is the life of the mind itself which is not mind except so far as it both lives in the historical process and knows itself as so living." These words have always impressed me as applicable to the core of the psychoanalytic method; and in preparation for Einstein's Centenary I attempted to formulate the way in which the psychoanalytic method of investigation both permits and demands a systematic awareness of a specific kind of relativity.

As to this very idea of relativity, all revolutionary advances in the natural sciences, of course, have cognitive and ethical implications that at first seem to endanger the previously dominant world image and with it the very cosmic reassurances of the basic dimensions of a sense of "I." Thus, to give only one example, Copernicus upset man's (as well as the earth's) central position in the universe that, no doubt, had been an arrangement supported by and in support of every I's natural sense of centeredness. But eventually, such multiple enlightenment as comes with a radical reorientation also reaffirms the adaptive power of the human mind and thus stimulates a more rational central and inventive ethos. Relativity, too, at first had unbearably relativistic implications, seemingly undermining the foundations of any firm human "standpoint"; and yet, it opens a new vista in which relative standpoints are "reconciled" to each other in fundamental invariance.

Comparably, Freud could pride himself on assigning to human consciousness a peripheral position on the very border of the "id," a cauldron of drives, for the energy of which (in a century most cognizant of nature's energy transformations) he claimed an "equal dignity." Now, as I pointed out in my Centenary address (1980b) Einstein and Freud themselves mistrusted each other's methods. Yet, it appears—or it appeared to me—that the principle of relativity, or, at any rate, one of Einstein's favorite illustrations of it (namely, the relation of two moving railroad cars to each other) can be applied to Freud's basic method.

The *psychoanalytic situation*, I claimed, can be reviewed in terms that picture the psychoanalyst's and the patient's minds at work as two "coordinate systems" moving relatively to each other. The seeming repose and impersonality of the psychoanalytic encounter actually permit and intensify in the patient a "free floating" of "associations" that can move about with varying speed through the distant past, or the immediate present, to the feared or wished-for future, and, at the same time, in the spheres of concrete experience, fantasy, and dream life. The patient suffers from symptoms betraying some arrest in the present and yet related to developmental fixations on one or more of the core pathologies characteristic of earlier stages of life. Free association, therefore, can be expected to induce the analysand to remember and to relive, if often in symbolically disguised form, conflicts intrinsic to previous stages and states of development. Their whole significance, however, often does not become clear until the patient reveals in his fantasies and thoughts a "transference" on the psychoanalyst's person of some of the revived and more or less irrational images and affects of earlier and earliest life periods.

The psychoanalyst, in turn, has undergone a "training psychoanalysis" that has taught him a kind of perpetual, but (at its

best) disciplined and unobtrusive, awareness of his own mind's
wanderings through developmental and historical time. Thus,
while viewing the patient's verbalizations in the light of what has
been learned of the general direction of his or her life, the psychoanalyst remains consistently ready to become aware of the
way in which the patient's present state and past conflicts reverberate in his or her *own* life situation and evoke feelings and images
from the corresponding stages of the past—in brief, the thera-
pist's "countertransference." Such complex interplay is not only
enlightening, it also helps to detect (and to learn from) any possible unconscious collusion of the listener's own habitual fantasies and denials with those of the patient.

But while thus moving about in their respective life cycles,
relative as they both are to different social and historical trends,
the practitioner's interpretive thoughts are also moving with the
past and current conceptualizations of psychoanalysis: including, of course, the analyst's own "generational" position between
his or her own training analysis and other influential training
personalities and schools; as well as his or her own intellectual
ruminations, intrinsically related as they are to one's development as a worker and as a person. And each old or new clinical
and theoretical model or "map" can, as we saw, be marked by
significant shifts in clinical ethos.

Only by having learned to remain potentially—and, as I said,
unobtrusively—aware of the relativity governing all these related
movements can the psychoanalyst hope to reach healing and
enlightening insights that may lead to interpretations fitting the
therapeutic moment. Such interpretations are often equally surprising, in their utter uniqueness and in their human lawfulness,
to both practitioner and client. In thus clarifying the patient's
course of life in the light of the given therapeutic encounter,
interpretation heals through an expansion of developmental and
historical insight.

And so I had the temerity to relate Einstein's and my own
field, as each participant was asked to do, at the Centenary cele-

bration in Jerusalem. It seemed to me that some such approach is an intrinsic part of a new method of observation that makes age-old empathy systematic and establishes a lawful interplay not otherwise accessible. As to its special clinical application, it is guided by a modern caritas that takes it for granted that the healer and the to-be-healed in principle share—and can share most actually—the invariant laws of human motivation as revealed by the relativities observed. At the same time, however, it is part of a new kind of life-historical and historical awareness that demands to be integrated into the ethos of modern man: whether it be intensely professionalized as in healing procedures, part of the workings of some related fields such as hitory, sociology, or political science, or indeed, simply entering gradually the insight of daily life.

This book began with some notes on my training in Vienna and especially on the spirit of the therapeutic enterprise. I think that I can best conclude by referring once more to the international congress of psychoanalysts in 1979 in New York. There, in addition to speaking on generativity (1980(c)) I also participated in a panel discussion on the relationship of transference and life cycle. The members of the panel were Peter Neubauer, Peter Blos, and Pearl King who, respectively, spoke on patterns of transference in children, in adolescents, and in adults—including the middle aged and the elderly (P. Blos; P. Newbauer; P. King; 1980). I can offer here only a few comments in line with our deliberations.

The classical difference between the psychoanalytic situation encountered in work with adults and with children has of course been the fact that children, in their immaturity of personality, are unable to recline and to introspect systematically. If anything, they want to interact, to play, and to converse. And so they prove unable to develop systematic transferences, not to speak of that artifact called "transference neurosis" that marks, most instructively, adult treatment. Now, it has always seemed to be a bit of adult chauvinism to complain about the inability of children to develop transference neuroses. How could they, and why should they, immersed as they are in experiencing the present and in trying to translate it into a playful self-expression with multiple learning functions. As for their infantile attachments, Anna Freud once remarked that the first edition is simply not sold out yet; otherwise she speaks only of "different transference reactions" (A. Freud, 1980, p. 2). And while there can be only occasional "transferences" of persistent symbiotic needs for early parental figures, it must be remembered that children must continue to learn to use other selected adults, be they grandparents or neighbors, doctors, or teachers, for much-needed extraparental encounters. Thus, what is sometimes monotonously referred to as the child patient's search for "*object-relations*" (that is, for a fully deserving and responding recipient of one's love) must come to include that clarified *mutuality of involvement* on which the life of generations depends. A child patient, in fact, may well be ready to comprehend something of the role of the analyst, or what Neubauer significantly calls the link between *transient transference* relations and a *working alliance* with the analyst. But could one not see another adult chauvinistic trend in the fact that in the discussion of transference in psychoanalytic work with children and adolescents we rarely consider in serious detail our unavoidable *countertransference* either in relation to the youngsters or, indeed, their parents?

What has been said about childhood appears in new and dramatic forms in adolescence. True, sexual maturation is now under way, but there is again a planned delay (we have called it a psychosocial latency) both in personality development and in social status that permits a period of experimentation with social roles by regressive recapitulations as well as experimental anticipations, often aggravated by an alternation of extremes. And again, the evolutionary logic of this is apparent in the fact that adolescence can lead to a psychosocial identity only as it finds its own outlines in "confirmations" and in gradual commitments to rudimentary friendship, love, partnership, and ideological association—in whatever order. Peter Blos speaks forcefully not only of a regression in the service of development but also of a *second individuation* process. As for the corresponding transference, Blos describes how "the adolescent patient *actively* constitutes, so to say, remodeled parental images; he thus creates ingenuously corrected new editions of old scripts via the analyst's presence as a real person" (1980). This obviously assigns to the analyst of adolescents the double position of one who heals by well-dosed interpretation and yet is also committed to the role of a generative model of cautious affirmation—a mentor, then. The patient's second individuation, in turn, must also mean a gradual capacity for friendships and associations that denote a respect for and recognition of the individuation of others and a mutual actualization of and by them.

As to the transferences evident in adult patients, however, it must once more be remembered that adults in general, unlike children and adolescents, must submit to the classical treatment setting. For it forces on the patient—as we can now appreciate in detail—a specific combination of (1) a supine position throughout (remember the importance of the upright posture in human encounters); (2) an avoidance of facial confrontation and of all eye-to-eye contact (remember the decisive importance of mutual recognition by glance and smile); (3) an exclusion of conversational give and take (remember the importance of conversation for a mutual delineation of the "I"); and, finally, (4) the endurance of the analyst's silence. All of this provokes ingeniously a nostalgic search through memory and transference for early infantile counterplayers. No wonder that the patient has to be relatively healthy (that is, reasonably tolerant of all these frustrations) to undergo such a cure. At the same time, of course, this whole arrangement imposes on the analyst an investiture with a healing authority that cannot be without influence on the countertransference and thus doubly demands analytic insight.

When discussing adults, Pearl King moved decisively to middle age—and beyond. There, she points out, individuals live by a variety of time standards: chronological, biological, and psychological. This threesome corresponds pretty well to our Ethos, Soma, and Psyche: for it is the Ethos that projects its values on chronological time, while Soma remains master of the biological, and Psyche of the experienced time. Of special interest for us (who in these pages began our stagewise approach with the last stage) is Pearl King's description of a reversal of transference in advanced years, which she formulates thus: "The analyst can be experienced in the transference as *any* significant figure from the patient's past, sometimes covering a span of five generations, and for any of these transference figures the roles may be reversed, so that the patient behaves to the analyst as he felt he was treated by them" (1980). And King does not omit the complex countertransference in relation to elderly patients: "The affects, whether positive or negative, that may accompany such transference phenomena are often very intense with older patients, and they may arouse unacceptable feelings in the analyst toward his own aging parents. It is therefore necessary for those undertaking the psychoanalysis of such patients to have come to terms with their own feelings about their own parents and to have accepted in a healthy, self-integrative way their own stage in their life cycle and their own aging process" (p. 185). King also suggests, as already mentioned, that it is often difficult for aging patients to contemplate a conclusion of their treatment: for then, it seems, they will be obliged to face the authority of the seemingly merciless process of time on its own terms.

In all stages of life, then, the patients' varying forms of transference seem to represent an attempt to involve the analyst as a generative being in the repetition of selected life crises in order to restore a previously broken *developmental dialogue*. The dynamics of this clinical encounter of the generations, however, can obviously not be fully clarified except by a study of the typical experiences of the psychoanalyst's countertransference in relation to patients of different ages. For, to quote myself, "only by remaining consistently open to the way in which the patient's present as well as past stages reverberate in the analyst's experience of the corresponding stages can the psychoanalyst become more fully aware of the generational implications of psychoanalytic work." I emphasize this in conclusion because I think that in these matters it would be rewarding to compare the interplay of transferences and countertransferences between analysands and analysts of given sexes and ages in different cultural and historical settings. Freud's revolutionary decision to make this interplay of transferences the central issue in the healing situation has made of psychoanalysis, clinical and "applied," the prime method for the study of the *developmental* and *historical relativity* in human experience. And only such study can confirm what is, indeed, invariantly human.

These concluding remarks on the basic psychoanalytic situation can do no more than illustrate what was said at the very beginning of this essay; namely, that to see what is most familiar in our daily work in terms of relativity (as well as complementarity) may do better justice to some aspects of psychoanalysis than some of the causal and quantitative terms that were of the essence to the theories of the founders. At any rate, it is evident that a psychosocial orientation fuses naturally with such a developmental and historical view, and that clinical observations made with such awareness in dealing with patients of different ages in different areas of the world can in the very process of healing serve to register the fate of the basic human strengths and core disturbances under changing technological and historical conditions. Thus, clinical work can supplement other ways of taking the pulse of changing history and in advancing an all-human awareness.

5

The Ninth Stage

INTRODUCTION

When the eight stages were initially charted, it seemed obvious that apart from the infant's arrival date such variety exists in the timing of human development that no age specifications could be validated for each stage independent of social criteria and pressures.

While this is also true of old age, it is useful to delineate a specific time frame in order to focus on the life experiences and crises of the period. Old age in one's eighties and nineties brings with it new demands, reevaluations, and daily difficulties. These concerns can only be adequately discussed, and confronted, by designating a new ninth stage to clarify the challenges. We must now see and understand the final life cycle stages through late-eighty- and ninety-year-old eyes.

Even the best cared-for bodies begin to weaken and do not function as they once did. In spite of every effort to maintain strength and control, the body continues to lose its autonomy. Despair, which haunts the eighth stage, is a close companion in the ninth because it is almost impossible to know what emergencies and losses of physical ability are imminent. As independence and control are challenged, self-esteem and confidence weaken. Hope and trust, which once provided firm support, are no longer the sturdy props of former days. To face down despair with faith and appropriate humility is perhaps the wisest course.

As I review the life cycle, and I have been doing so for a long time, I realize that the eight stages are most often presented with the syntonic quotient mentioned first, followed by the dystonic element second—e.g., trust vs. mistrust; autonomy vs. shame and doubt, etc. The syntonic supports growth and expansion, offers goals, celebrates self-respect and commitment of the very finest. Syntonic qualities sustain us as we are challenged by the more dystonic elements with which life confronts us all. We should recognize the fact that circumstances may place the dystonic in a more dominant position. Old age is inevitably such a circumstance. In writing "The Ninth Stage," I have therefore placed the dystonic element first in order to underscore its prominence and potency. In either case, it is important to remember that conflict and tension are sources of growth, strength, and commitment.

With the chart of the stages well in mind, and perhaps helpfully before you, let us review stage by stage what the aged individual faces of the syntonic and dystonic elements and the tensions with which he or she must cope. Let us face the disturbing dystonic potentials of the stages and give them full attention and consideration as they appear to individuals in the ninth stage.

BASIC MISTRUST VS. TRUST: HOPE

Lucky the infants who come into this world with good genes, loving parents, and even grandparents who readily relate to them enthusiastically and enjoy them hugely. We must acknowledge the fact that without basic trust the infant cannot survive. It follows that every living person has basic trust and with it, to some degree, the strength of hope. Basic trust is the confirmation of hope, our consistent buttress against all the trials and so-called tribulations of life in this world. Although survival would be difficult without a modicum of mistrust to protect us, mistrust can contaminate all aspects of our lives and deprive us of love and fellowship with human beings.

Elders are forced to mistrust their own capabilities. Time takes its toll even on those who have been healthy and able to maintain sturdy muscles, and the body inevitably weakens. Hope may easily give way to despair in the face of continual and increasing disintegration, and in light of both chronic and sudden indignities. Even the simple activities of daily living may present difficulty and conflict. No wonder elders become tired and often depressed. Yet elders readily accept that the sun goes down at night and rejoice to see it rise brightly every morning. While there is light, there is hope, and who knows what bright light and revelation any morning may bring?

SHAME AND DOUBT VS. AUTONOMY: WILL

Surely all parents remember how, when their children were quite young, two years of age or so, they became surprisingly willful, grasping spoons and toys, ready to stand up on their own feet. Their stance is playful but firm and self-satisfying. They will to do, and they demonstrate that they can. The stronger the will, the more they undertake. Since growth happens so fast and with such satisfaction, parents can only wonder and hope for their success. But there are limits; when these are overstepped and things get out of control, there may be a reversion to insecurity and a lack of self-confidence that ends in shame and doubt in their capacities.

Something of this doubt returns to elders as they no longer trust in their autonomy over their bodies and life choices. Will becomes weakened, though held in check enough to provide some security and to avoid the shame of lost self-control. One wills what is safe and sound, and nothing is quite safe, for sure.

Autonomy. Remember how it feels, how it always felt, to want everything your way. I suspect this drive continues to our last breath. When you were young, all the elders were stronger and more powerful; now the powerful are younger than you. When you are feisty and stubborn about arrangements made for or about you, all the more powerful elements—doctors, lawyers, and your own grown children—get into the act. They may well be right, but it can make you feel rebellious. Shame and doubt challenge cherished autonomy.

GUILT VS. INITIATIVE: PURPOSE

To initiate suggests a moving out into a new direction. It may be a lonely trip and still be successful, or it may be a move that catches the interest and participation of others. Initiative is brave and valiant, but when it misfires, a strong sense of deflation follows. It is lively and enthusiastic while it lasts, but the initiative instigator is often left with a sense of inadequacy and guilt.

Elders who took leadership seriously early in life may in later years shun the guilt that accompanies overzealous initiative. While once you were full of creative ideas, at eighty plus it's all memorable enthusiasm. At a distance it seems too much and not centered. The sense of purpose and the enthusiasm are dulled; there is plenty to do in just keeping up with a slow, constant, demanding pace. Guilt raises its ugly head when an elder is too bent in carrying out some project that seems utterly satisfying and appealing—but only personally.

INFERIORITY VS. INDUSTRY: COMPETENCE

Industry and competence are aptitudes we all know about in this competitive country, this land of the free and home of the innovative. What are you good at, what are you good for are the first queries of a fellow human being. Our schools start us off that way, and we seldom recover the playfulness that led into original creativity. We all are graded on our competence.

Writing is a good example of our evaluation of competence. One may have splendid ideas, perhaps even the capacity to illustrate a new version of an old idea, but without the competence to write clearly and speak accurately, one would surely be classified as incompetent. In truth everything one does or attempts to do demands a standard of competence in order to be acceptable and understandable. It is not necessary to be original or inventive, but it is mandatory to be competent in order to excel in our practical world.

The industry that was a driving force when you were in your forties is a memory you may hardly recall. You were so proud of your competence. Such energy! That urgency is gone, and very likely that's a blessing because you really don't have enough strength for the pace you set then. But when the challenge pushes you on, you are forced to accept your inadequacy. Not to be competent because of aging is belittling. We become like unhappy small children of great age.

IDENTITY CONFUSION VS. IDENTITY: FIDELITY

Identity marks, acclaims, and distinguishes each infant at birth and is immediately confirmed by naming. A boy gets a boy's name, and likewise a girl's name pronounces her to be female. There are any number of names that we can then respond to or disavow. The greatest problem we encounter is who we think we are vs. who others may think we are or are trying to be. Who does he or she think I am? is a troublesome question to ask oneself, and it is difficult to find the appropriate answer.

We play roles, of course, and try out for parts we wish we could play for real, especially as we explore in adolescence. Costumes and makeup may sometimes be persuasive, but in the long run it is only having a genuine sense of who we are that keeps our feet on the ground and our heads up to an elevation from which we can see clearly where we are, what we are, and what we stand up for.

To be confused about this existential identity makes you a riddle to yourself and to many, perhaps even most, other people. With aging, you may feel a real uncertainty about status and role. By what names in your old age do you wish to be called? How independent can you afford to be? Who are you at eighty-five and beyond, when compared with who you were at midlife? Your role is unclear when compared with the firmness of your earlier stance and purpose. In fact, you may be confused about what role, what position you are supposed to take in this period when older values are suddenly vague and crumbling.

ISOLATION VS. INTIMACY: LOVE

The years of intimacy and love are bright and full of warmth and sunlight. To love and find oneself in another is to bring fulfillment and delight. Adding offspring to the circle is joyous enrichment. To see them grow and become qualified to take hold of their own lives is wonderful and gratifying.

Everyone is not so lucky and so blessed. A sense of isolation and deprivation attacks those for whom this rich period is not realized. The aging elder may no doubt feel very isolated and left out if life has not brought him or her such riches to remember and relish. If in old age no such memories are tucked away for reevoking with photograph or remembered story, there instead may be a total devotion to art, literature, or scholarship to offset these losses. Some individuals are happily and completely devoted to their work, their calling and creativity.

All elders in the ninth stage may be unable to depend on the ways in which they are used to relating with others. How one typically engages and makes contact with others may be overshadowed by new incapacities and dependencies. Older individuals may need to initiate interaction more often since others may feel insecure or uncomfortable, unsure of how to "break the ice." Awkwardness, resulting from confusion about how to interact with someone who is not "like everybody else," may leave many elders deprived of potential connection and intimate exchange. To add to the confusion, an elder's community of others may shrink or expand depending on circumstance; at the very least it will change frequently.

STAGNATION VS. GENERATIVITY: CARE

The stage of generativity claims the longest stretch of time on the chart—thirty years or more, during which one establishes a working commitment and perhaps begins a new family, devoting time and energy to furthering its healthy and productive life. During this period work and family relationships confront one with the duties of caretaking and a widening range of obligations and responsibilities, interests, and celebrations. When this is satisfactorily cohesive, all can go well and prosper. It's a wonderful time to be alive, cared for and caring, surrounded by those nearest and dearest. It is challenging, exciting at best, though burdensome if rigid and demanding. One may also become involved in the community and many of its diverse activities. This involvement can be inundating, but it is never dull.

Toward the end of this demanding period one may feel an urge to withdraw somewhat, only to experience a loss of the stimulus of belonging, of being needed. At eighty or ninety one may begin to have less energy, less capacity to adjust quickly to the abruptness of the changes being imposed by the busy bodies all around. Generativity, which comprised the major life involvement of active individuals, is no longer necessarily expected in old age. This releases elders from the assignment of caretaking. However, not being needed may be felt as a designation of uselessness. When no challenges are offered, a sense of stagnation may well take over. Others, of course, may welcome this as a promise of respite, but if one should withdraw altogether from generativity, from creativity, from caring for and with others entirely, that would be worse than death.

DESPAIR AND DISGUST VS. INTEGRITY: WISDOM

In our final definition of "wisdom" we claim that wisdom rests in the capacity to see, look, and remember, as well as to listen, hear, and remember. Integrity, we maintain, demands tact, contact, and touch. This is a serious demand on the senses of elders. It takes a lifetime to learn to be tactful and demands both patience and skill; it is all too easy to become weary and discouraged. It is a serious challenge at ninety just to locate misplaced eyeglasses. Ninth stage elders just do not usually have the adequately good eyesight or the receptive ears wisdom demands, although we may rejoice in the progress being made with hearing devices and eye surgery.

In encounters between the syntonic and dystonic, the dystonic elements win out as time goes on; despair is "in attendance." Ninth stage despair reflects a somewhat different experience from that affiliated with the eighth stage. Life in the eighth stage includes a retrospective accounting of one's life to date; how much one embraces life as having been well lived, as opposed to regretting missed opportunities, will contribute to the degree of disgust and despair one experiences. As Erik has reminded us, "Despair expresses the feeling that the time is now short, too short for the attempt to start another life and to try out alternate roads. . . ."*

In one's eighties and nineties one may no longer have the luxury of such retrospective despair. Loss of capacities and disintegration may demand almost all of one's attention. One's focus may become thoroughly circumscribed by concerns of daily functioning so that it is enough just to get through a day intact, however satisfied or dissatisfied one feels about one's previous life history. Of course despair in response to these more immediate and acute events is compounded by earlier self and life evaluations.

An elder in his or her eighties or nineties is also apt to have experienced many losses, some of distant relationships and some of more profound and close relationships—parents, partners, and even children. There is much sorrow to cope with plus a clear announcement that death's door is open and not so far away.

Should you be living and coping with all these hurdles and losses at ninety or more, you have one firm foothold to depend on. From the beginning we are blessed with basic trust. Without it life is impossible, and with it we have endured. As an enduring strength it has accompanied and bolstered us with hope. Whatever the specific sources of our basic trust may be or have been, and no matter how severely hope has been challenged, it has never abandoned us completely. Life without it is simply unthinkable. If you still are filled with the intensity of being and hope for what may be further grace and enlightenment, then you

---

* *Childhood and Society*, p. 269.

have reason for living. I am persuaded that if elders can come to terms with the dystonic elements in their life experiences in the ninth stage, they may successfully make headway on the path leading to gerotranscendence.

As Erik has often pointed out, an individual life cycle cannot be adequately understood apart from the social context in which it comes to fruition. Individual and society are intricately woven, dynamically interrelated in continual exchange. Erik notes: "Lacking a culturally viable ideal of old age, our civilization does not really harbor a concept of the whole of life." As a result, our society does not truly know how to integrate elders into its primary patterns and conventions or into its vital functioning. Rather than be included, aged individuals are often ostracized, neglected, and overlooked; elders are seen no longer as bearers of wisdom but as embodiments of shame. Recognizing that the difficulties of the ninth stage both contribute to and are exacerbated by society's disregard, let us now turn to a more detailed consideration of the interplay between elders and their society.

6

Old Age and Community

ONE OF THE delightful experiences of elders is to have forthright conversations with grandchildren. As I picked blueberries with Christopher one sunny day down on the Cape, we congratulated ourselves on the dandy job we were doing. He could effectively clear the lower branches within his reach, while I was busy with the upper levels of the bushes. No berries eluded us, and our baskets were getting very full. After a while I did need to sit down on a rock and rest a bit, but not he. He continued for a moment or so and then stood up very straight in front of me to clarify essentials. "Nama," he said, "you are old and I am new"—an unchallengeable pronouncement.

In our country useless old things, as we know, are taken to the dump. We have, however, introduced "recycling," which extends the usefulness of old objects for a while and keeps us from overburdening the land with enduring deposits of debris. We don't take our old folks to the dump, but we certainly don't do enough toward their recycling. What if we could make available to elders better eye care, more eyeglasses, and more hearing aids and provide them with large-print magazines and papers, as well as large-print books? All health care advisers promote exercise, at least regular walking schedules, to maintain health and mobility. But few towns and cities maintain safe sidewalks and streets where elders can move slowly and cautiously. Have you ever seen a town in this country where occasional benches are provided so that an elderly shopper can take a breather or relax a moment in the process of carrying home the shopping bag or bundle?

As my life proceeds into the misnamed area of the eighth and last stages, I begin to wonder about the unexpected experiences and observations that consistently confront me. The usual attitude toward elders in our society is bewildering. While historical, anthropological, and religious documents record that long-lived elders of ancient times were applauded and even revered, this century's response to aged individuals is often derision, words of contempt, and even revulsion. If help is offered, it tends to be overdone. Pride is wounded, and respect is in jeopardy. The aged are offered a totally playless second childhood. If an elder can't climb stairs readily or weaves as he or she walks, this misfortune is equated with a loss of thinking and remembering. It is often easier to give in to these verdicts than to defy them. The deaf and blind have found *some* ways to cope with their deprivations and to maintain their human right to live out their lives in the privacy of their own feelings, judgment, and pace. They have profited from fine institutions dedicated to their support.

Suppose that you have learned that knowing yourself is true wisdom and opens your ears and eyes. How does that knowledge alone prepare you for the last long trek to death's door? What does our society do to facilitate the transitions of the last life cycle stages and to adapt to the presence of elders? The whole population is growing older. There are more people over eighty than ever before, and medicine is making great strides to increase the life-span. As yet, however, no program of how to incorporate elders into our society and living arrangements has been adequately envisioned and designed.

When, in this country and especially in our crowded cities, we began to consider how we could support and care for our elders, we made a giant step forward. It was clear that elders often need twenty-four-hour care. A few residential care facilities were undertaken within city limits, but cities are crowded and noisy, and the air is polluted. Some effort was made to find appropriate housing in the suburbs. That was an improvement, but soon it became obvious that land outside town and suburbia was plentiful, cheaper, and in many ways more practical. Large areas were appropriated, carefully laid out, and built up. Many of these developments are set in beautiful surroundings and offer thoughtfully planned schedules of entertainment as well as excellent care and supervision. The places selected for such facilities often include beautiful trees and ponds, making charming short walks available for "inmates." That these homes for the elderly are planned to serve their needs in every way is obvious, and thus beyond debate and criticism, except that the cost is high, much too high for most.

In general we find that the larger the residential facility, the more specialized and segregated the staff becomes. Many must be on call all night. Vacations and overworking of staff often result in high rates of turnover followed by the initial ineptness of new help. Since most of the personnel live outside the compound, large parking areas often surround the whole enterprise. Trucks bring food and drink, office equipment, clothing, and entertainment. Hairdressers come by schedule, as do foot specialists, dentists, manicurists, and masseurs. The kitchen staff arrives and departs; the serving staff likewise, and the cleaning contingent functions early in order to be ready to receive "inmates" and guests. In this regard a facility is run like a big hotel. There are activity programs daily under the auspices of the activities director or committee. Sabbath services and special events and holidays are regularly planned by the staff. Probably "inmates" have an opportunity to convey their hopes and wishes for special activities; bingo is often very popular. There is an enormous diversity of activity and time spent on caretaking and quality. The fact that so much good work is accomplished is remarkable and commendable.

Then there are the elders, for whom all this was devised, and their doctors and nurses. The elders may be slowed-down, insecure, or temporarily helpless. Many need wheelchairs, walkers, or canes;

some are incontinent; some have dietary problems; many have broken, unhealed bones. These are fragile communities at best. Continuity of interrelationships and daily functioning are continually threatened by any and all unexpected breakdowns in the systemic "machinery" and by shifts in the population of the served and the serving.

Something is terribly wrong. Why has it been necessary to send our elders "out of this world" into some facility so remote in order to live out their lives in physical care and comfort? Every human being is headed for old age, with all its joys and sorrows. But how can we learn from our elders how to prepare for the end of life, which we all must face alone, if our role models do not live among us? One solution, though probably only a dream, would be for every city to have parks—fine, well-guarded parks—available to all. In the middle of each park could be a residence for elders. When able, they could take short walks or rides in wheelchairs within the park with their relatives and close friends, who could also visit, sit, and talk with them on terraces and decks. We all could speak to them and hear their stories, learning what they still have to offer of their wisdom.

Let's say we have made it through the eighth stage with major and minor losses of friends and relatives. Physical strength and capacities have slowly but inevitably let us down. Most of us have not been living in close contact with friends or relatives who have lived into their nineties, so we have not fully shared their experience of what life becomes in the ninth stage. How can we plan or imagine how to conform to this unknown future and make it as rich, meaningful, and stimulating as possible? With what stories of successful aging do we alert and inform ourselves on our way? Perhaps elders over ninety should meet together to compare new experiences and make enjoyable short-range plans. They should share some of the benefits and satisfactions of feeling free to let involvement with the youth of the world slacken and become less attractive.

I remember seeing older men in the streets of southern Europe sitting on benches outside their houses, smoking pipes, chatting and joking, watching the world go by. The women were indoors, gossiping probably; they speak another language from the men, though they surely enjoy it equally well spiced. In China, India, and Tibet, we are informed, the old wise men often settle into caves and enjoy whatever nourishment their younger admirers and students bring them. Solitude does not dismay them, and visits inspire, strengthen, and make life worthwhile.

In our northern Arctic wilds, appropriate patterns have been devised. If Eskimos travel to distant areas as communities in order to find better hunting or fishing, they set out with sleds and dogs, equipment, and enough food for all. No stopping for any length of time is possible; the cold is cruel. Should an aged one not be able to keep up, an igloo must be fashioned with ice—big enough for one. He or she will be settled in and left behind. That person will understand and know in advance that this is a potential farewell and will probably wish it so. To freeze to death is better than to hold back and jeopardize the whole community. No doubt people prepare throughout their lives for this eventuality. Where this necessity is understood, elders are celebrated and revered. All can take part in venerating the occasion and the elder. In our culture we perhaps don't have enough faith and trust in the community to dedicate such dignified and honoring celebrations of passage.

We seem to have no appropriate word, gesture, song, or stance for that final farewell, though we all seem to know that grievous dirge:

> You've got to cross that lonesome valley
> You've got to cross it by yourself
> There ain't no one going to cross it for you
> You've got to cross it by yourself.

Must we be so dull and dreary? What about all the animals and all the sentient creatures that died as you were dying? With no more hunger to fear, wouldn't we be ready to share that valley with all: running, crawling, standing, flying, dancing, making appropriate sounds of release, laughter, bellowing, singing, fearless and curious, free and transcendent?

In the past year I have had the opportunity to be with and observe a number of older people who are not up to "making it" in family life in general. They need the special care and help of a nursing facility. I observe with what difficulty they walk, even with the support of canes and walkers, how awkward standing up straight is, how precarious sitting down has become. The spring, the rhythm have left their bodies. Falling down is a perpetual threat with its hazard of getting hurt and its challenge, both awkward and demoralizing, of getting up again from way down on the floor. How they manage is a constant wonder—a caution to younger people who are facing life's trials and troubles more advantageously.

Where in limited, repetitive, daily lives do these "retired" and resigned elders find refreshment and stimulus, some joy or the nurturing of soul and sense necessary for survival? Surely the spectacular beauty of nature and changing seasons, in matters both large and small, consistently surprises and stimulates us all. The arts have always played their role; beauty, song, and the response of all the senses remain and can be counted on, called upon, and absorbed. Religious groups offer and provide abiding support to their members and the needy who seek them out. Families do what they can to support ongoing relationships; they extend what help and warmth are possible. When distance precludes their involvement, organizations such as Hospice move in vigorously to the rescue of the isolated who let their needs be known.

What, we may ask, would be a special approach to look to for relating with elders? How can we express more grace and refined acuity than we often are able to muster for the meeting of hearts, senses, and minds? In one way we have practically known the answer without actually understanding its meaning. When we are faced with a really troublesome problem, we sometimes resort to putting the matter "in the hands of" those more knowledgeable than ourselves. That is of course precisely what an ideal health care institution offers: hands, understanding, capable, talented hands, which have had careful training and much experience in communication with those who are limited in their modes of expressing needs. "In the hands of"—nothing could state more clearly what the importance of hands is and must be for patients everywhere. Conscious and attentive use of the hands would make all our lives more meaningful in the care and comfort of relationships with patients who feel isolated and somewhat abandoned. Hands are essential for vital involvement in living.

I am persuaded that if retired elders could have regular, if not daily, massage, it would be amazingly beneficial, refreshing, and relaxing. We need to be mindful of the distinction between maintenance touch—that is, touch in the service of hygiene and management (e.g., wiping, lifting, feeding)—and communicative touch—that is, touch in the service of human connection (e.g., rubbing the back and shoulders, holding a hand). Even maintenance touch can be provided with a respectful and humanizing regard that leaves patients feeling that they are being treated as people, not as objects to be tidied and transported.

7

Gerotranscendence

IN THE PURSUIT of following how aged people face the deterioration of their bodies and faculties, gerotricians have begun to use the word "transcendence" to describe a state that some aging persons develop and retain. Let me quote, to begin, the definition of the word "gerotranscendence" presented by Lars Tornstam and fellow workers at Uppsala Universitet, Sweden:

> With points of departure from our own studies as well as from theories and observations from others . . . we suggest that human aging, the very process of living into old age, encompasses a general potential towards gerotranscendence. Simply put, gerotranscendence is a shift in meta perspective, from a materialistic and rational vision to a more cosmic and transcendent one, normally followed by an increase in life satisfaction. Depending on the definition of "religion," the theory of gerotranscendence may or may not be regarded as a theory of religious development. In a study of terminal patients Nystrom and Andersson-Segesten (1990) found a condition, peace of mind, in some of the patients. This condition is in many ways close to our concept of gerotranscendence. They did not, however, find any correlation between this state of mind and the existence of a religious belief or religious practice in the patients. Regardless of this, the patients had or had not reached the state of peace of mind. . . . As in Jung's theory of the individuation process, gerotranscendence is regarded as the final stage in a natural process towards maturation and wisdom. It defines a reality somewhat different from

the normal mid-life reality which gerontologists tend to project on old age. According to the theory, the gerotranscendent individual experiences a new feeling of cosmic communion with the spirit of the universe, a redefinition of time, space, life and death, and a redefinition of the self. This individual might also experience a decrease in interest in material things and a greater need for solitary "meditation."*

These theorists continue this discussion with comments of various gerontologists, the contributions of Zen Buddhist theory, and other contributors from a variety of disciplines.

The statement in the quoted report describes what the gerotranscendent individual experiences—namely:

1. "There is new feeling of cosmic communion with the spirit of the universe," regarding which I refer the reader to Lewis Thomas's *The Lives of a Cell.*

2. Time is circumscribed to now, or maybe next week, for probably anyone over ninety; beyond that the vista is misty.

3. Space has slowly decreasing dimensions within the radius of our physical capabilities.

4. Death becomes syntonic, the way of all living things.

5. One's sense of self expands to include a wider range of interrelated others.

"Transcendence" is a word one is reluctant to use freely, for it has the tone, the imprint of the special, the holy. According to the dictionary, "to transcend" simply means "to rise above or go beyond a limit, exceed, excel"; also "to go beyond the universe and time." "Transcendence" has placed itself in the domain of religion, where it is on holy ground and protected from casual usage. That the word is used in all religions is unsurprising since it covers an area passing human knowledge, while expressing the hopes and expectations of all true believers.

*L. Tornstam, "Gerotranscendence: A Theoretical and Empirical Exploration," in L. E. Thomas and S. A. Eisenhandler, eds. *Aging and the Religious Dimension* (Westport, Conn.: Greenwood Publishing Group, 1993).

Historians of earlier epochs present evidence of how in the Orient the aged were held in high esteem for long lives of service and good judgment. Wise elders were applauded for leaving the bustle of community life, retreating into the mountains and remote places to live out their lives. Though the retreat may have been lonely, it did not cost them self-respect, and many were fed and cared for adequately enough to allow for years of retirement. I am told that even spiritual leaders in many areas of the world have responded with physical withdrawal from the overbusy schedules of monasteries and convents.

Perhaps the really old find a safe place to consider their states of being only in privacy and solitude. After all, how else can one find peace and acceptance of the changes that time imposes on mind and body? The race and competition are over and done with; to release oneself from hurry and tension is mandatory in old age. Some learn this early, and some too late.

This type of "withdrawal," in which one deliberately retreats from the usual engagements of daily activity, is consciously chosen withdrawal. Such a stance does not necessarily imply a lack of vital involvement; there may be continued involvement despite disengagement—as Erik says, a "deeply involved, disinvolvement." This paradoxical state does seem to exhibit a transcendent quality, a "shift . . . from a materialistic and rational vision." However, when withdrawal and retreat are motivated by a disdain for life and others, it is unlikely that such peace of mind and transcendence will be experienced.

Fortunate are those who have the luxury to choose to withdraw. Many elders are faced with enforced withdrawals. Physical deterioration of eyes, ears, teeth, bones, all the body's systems often inflicts an inevitable reduction in contact with others and the outside world. Emotional and psychological responses to decline may also inhibit one's range of contact. Of course this is all compounded by society, which often places elders where they are rarely seen or heard. The differences between chosen and imposed withdrawal in the orbit of a nursing facility are clear. If loss of physical aptitude occurs, the patient may naturally shift in attitude; a major improvement in physical abilities could also reverse an imposed withdrawal. Transcendence in the face of imposed withdrawal is perhaps less likely, though certainly not impossible.

In efforts to construct a socially effective sense of self in old age, we are tested on our *time identity*. We look toward a good future moment in order to escape the burden of the present. The normal societal model for old age has been to encourage letting go, but *not* to seek a new life and role—a new self. This promotion of false old age, or denial, stifles normal development. What should normal psychic development from maturity to death be? Is there seldom enough courage to confront aging selves without delusion? Just to seem younger and look younger is playacting. The wisdom of humility, which can be endless and strangely strong, is seldom encouraged. Intent on perfection and measuring up to expectations, we shy away as amateurs from "lovemaking" in creative activity and imagination.

In truth we are called to become more and more human; we must discover the freedom to go beyond limits imposed on us by our world and seek fulfillment. In the beginning we are what we are given. By midlife, when we have finally learned to stand on our own two feet, we learn that to complete our lives, we are called to give to others so that when we leave this world, we can be what we have given. Death, from this perspective, can be made our final gift. We believe it daily, but is it not possible, that by *living* our lives, we create something fit to add to the store from which we came? As Florida Maxwell has reminded us, our whole duty may be to clarify and increase what we are, to make our consciousness a finer quality. The effort of one's entire life would be needed to return laden to our source.

All too often when gerontologists use the term "gerotranscendence," they do not specify as clearly as possible all that they might describe. They do not take full account of those compensations that old age leaves behind. Nor do they sufficiently explore new and positive spiritual gifts. Perhaps they are just too young. I am still eager in my old age to activate words that sound a bit ethereal in order to make them lively components of behavior. With great satisfaction I have found that "transcendence" becomes very much alive if it is activated into "transcen*dance*," which speaks to soul and body and challenges it to rise above the dystonic, clinging aspects of our worldly existence that burden and distract us from true growth and aspiration.

To reach for gerotranscen*dance* is to rise above, exceed, outdo, go beyond, independent of the universe and time. It involves surpassing all human knowledge and experience. How, for heaven's sake, is this to be accomplished? I am persuaded that only by doing and making do we become. Transcendence need not be limited solely to experiences of withdrawal. In touching, we make contact with one another and with our planet. Transcen*dance* may be a regaining of lost skills, including play, activity, joy, and song, and, above all, a major leap above and beyond the fear of death. It provides an opening forward into the unknown with a trusting leap. Oddly enough, this all demands of us an honest and steadfast humility.

These are wonderful words, words that wind us up into involvement. Transcen*dance*—that's it, of course! And it moves. It's one of the arts, it's alive, sings, and makes music, and I hug myself because of the truth it whispers to my soul. No wonder writing has been so difficult. Transcen*dance* calls forth the languages of the arts; nothing else speaks so deeply and meaningfully to our hearts and souls. The great dance of life can transport us into all realms of making and doing with every item of body, mind, and spirit involved. I am profoundly moved, for I am growing old and feel shabby, and suddenly great riches present themselves and enlighten every part of my body and reach out to beauty everywhere. Somewhere Keats must be musing and smiling:

Beauty is truth, truth beauty—that is all
You know on earth, and all you need to know.

To grow old is a great privilege. It allows feedback on a long
life that can be relived in retrospect. With the years, retrospect
becomes more inclusive; scene and action become more real and
present. Sometimes the distant scenes and experiences are close
to bewildering, and to relive them in memory is almost overwhelming. With mind and heart set on retrospect, it is natural in
the ninth stage to find oneself on the upward course of a steep
hill. The path up this steep hill, to the vantage point where we
can greet the rising and setting sun, is narrow and littered with
rocks and rubbish, but every step rewards and draws us up
higher. With every step too the view stretches out its releasing
display, and the sky and the clouds perform their slow and gracious maneuvers.

But with all this fine talk you still may have your obligations
to the body that makes possible this climbing of the mountain,
whatever its demands may be. So the pack on your back must
also be considered, and, before that, the consistent care necessary
to keep the body machinery functioning appropriately in spite of
the age and deterioration of the original model. I do believe that
in the ninth stage it is mandatory to lighten our load of posses-
sions, especially those that call for supervision and care. If you
hope to climb the mountain, whether or not meditation beckons
you, travel must be light and unburdened. A lifetime of training
is required for success. It's so easy to blame the terrain, the light,
the wind for failures and backsliding. Moments of rest are mandatory, but there is no time for self-pity and weakening of purpose.
Light too is necessary, for the way and the days are all too short.
Song is joyous in the half-light. The dark offers release and
dreams of those near and dear and much beloved.

And so you set your course with your face to the rising sun,
your eyes alert for the slippery loose stones, your breath reluctant
to maintain the pace. You are forced to slow down and reconfirm

your decision to proceed. Always the syntonic and dystonic impulses, to proceed or to give in, wrestle for control and the will to make good. You are challenged and tested. This tension, when it is focused and controlled, is the very root of success. Every step is a test of syntonic sovereignty and will power.

References

Benedek, T. "Parenthood as a developmental phase." *Journal of the American Psychoanalytic Association* 7 (1959): 389–417.

Blos, P. "The second individuation process of adolescence." *The Psychoanalytic Study of the Child* 22 (1967): 162–86.

———"The life cycle as indicated by the nature of the transference in the psychoanalysis of adolescents." *International Journal of Psycho-Analysis* 61 (1980): 145–50.

Collingwood, R. G. *The Idea of History.* New York: Oxford University Press, 1956.

Einstein, A. *Ideas and Opinions.* New York: Crown Publishers, 1954.

Erikson, E. H. "Bilderbücher. *Zeitschrift für Psychoanalytische Paedagogik* 5 (1931): 417–45.

———"Configurations in play—clinical notes." *Psychoanalytic Quarterly* 6 (1937): 139–214.

———"Freud's "The Origins of Psychoanalysis." *International Journal of Psycho-Analysis* 36 (1955): 1–15.

———*Young Man Luther: A Study in Psychoanalysis and History.* New York: W.W. Norton, 1958.

———*Identity and the Life Cycle.* New York: W. W. Norton, 1980.

———*Childhood and Society.* New York: W.W. Norton, 1951; revised 1963.

———*Insight and Responsibility.* New York: W.W. Norton, 1964.

———*Gandhi's Truth.* New York: W.W. Norton, 1969.

———*Dimensions of a New Identity: The 1973 Jefferson Lectures.* New York: W.W. Norton, 1974.

132   References

——— *Toys and Reasons: Stages in the Ritualization of Experience.* New York: W.W. Norton, 1977.

——— *Life History and the Historical Moment.* New York: W.W. Norton, 1978.

——— "Elements of a psychoanalytic theory of psychosocial development. In *The Course of Life, Psychoanalytic Contributions Toward Understanding Personality Development*, edited by S. I. Greenspan and G. H. Pollack. Washington, D.C.: U.S. Government Printing Office, 1980(a).

——— "Psychoanalytic reflections on Einstein's Centenary." In: *Einstein and Humanism.* New York: Aspen Institute for Humanistic Studies, 1980(b).

——— "On the generational cycle: an address." *International Journal of Psycho-Analysis* 61 (1980(c)): 213–22.

——— "The Galilean sayings and the sense of 'I'." *Yale Review* Spring (1981): 321–62.

Erikson, J. M. "Eye to eye." In *The Man-Made Object*, edited by G. Kepes. New York: Braziller, 1966.

——— (with Erik H. Erikson) "Growth and crises of the 'healthy personality.' " In *Symposium on the Healthy Personality*, edited by M. Senn. New York: Josiah Macy Foundation, 1950.

——— *Activity—Recovery—Growth, The Communal Role of Planned Activity.* New York: W.W. Norton, 1976.

Erikson, K. T. *Wayward Puritans.* New York: Wiley, 1966.

Freud, A. "The concept of development lines." *The Psychoanalytic Study of the Child* 18:245–65, 1963.

——— *Normality and Pathology in Childhood: Assessments of Development.* New York: International Universities Press, 1965.

——— *The Ego and the Mechanisms of Defense* (1936). New York: International Universities Press, 1966.

——— "Child analysis as the study of mental growth (normal and abnormal)." In *The Course of Life: Psychoanalytic Contributions Toward Understanding Personality Development*, vol. 1, *Infancy and Early Childhood*, edited by S. I. Greenspan and G. H. Pollack. Washington, D.C.: U.S. Government Printing Office, 1980.

Freud, S. "On narcissism: An introduction" (1914). *Standard Edition*, 14:67–102. London: Hogarth Press; New York: W.W. Norton, 1957.

——— *The Origins of Psychoanalysis. Letters to Wilhelm Fliess, Drafts and Notes: 1887–1902.* Edited by Bonaparte. M.: Freud, A.: and Kris, E. London: Imago, 1954. New York: Basic Books, 1954.

——— "Group psychology and the analysis of the ego" (1921). *Standard Edition*, 18:69–143. London: Hogarth Press; New York, W.W. Norton, 1955.

——— "The ego and the id" (1923). *Standard Edition*, 19:12–66. London: Hogarth Press; New York: W.W. Norton, 1961.

References   133

——"Civilization and its discontents" (1930[1929]). *Standard Edition*, 21:59–145. London: Hogarth Press; New York: W.W. Norton, 1961.

——"New introductory lectures on psycho-analysis" (1933). *Standard Edition*, 22:7–182. London: Hogarth Press; New York: W.W. Norton, 1964.

Greenspan, S. I. "An integrated approach to intelligence and adaptation: A synthesis of psychoanalytic and Piagetian developmental psychology." *Psychological Issues*. Vols. 3 and 4. New York: International Universities Press, 1979.

Greenspan, S. I. and Pollock, G. H., eds. *The Course of Life: Psychoanalytic Contributions Toward Understanding Personality Development*. Vol. 1: *Infancy and Early Childhood*. Washington, D.C.: U.S. Government Printing Office, 1980.

Hartmann, H. *Ego Psychology and the Problem of Adaptation* (1939). Translated by David Rapaport. New York: International Universities Press, 1958.

——"Notes on the reality principle." *The Psychoanalytic Study of the Child* 11 (1956): 31–53.

——"On rational and irrational actions." *Psychoanalysis and the Social Sciences*, Vol. 1. New York: International Universities Press, 1947.

Huxley, J. *From An Antique Land: Ancient and Modern in the Middle East*. New York: Harper and Row, 1966.

James, W. *The Letters of William James*. Edited by H. James. Boston: Atlantic Monthly Press, 1920.

Jones, E. *The Life and Work of Sigmund Freud*. London: Hogarth Press, 1953; New York: Basic Books, 1953.

Kakar, S. *The Inner World: A Psychoanalytic Study of Hindu Childhood and Society*. New Delhi and New York: Oxford University Press, 1977.

King, P. "The life cycle as indicated by the nature of the transference in the psychoanalysis of the middle-aged and elderly." *International Journal of Psycho-Analysis* 61 (1980): 153–59.

Knox, B. *Oedipus at Thebes*. New York: W.W. Norton, 1957.

Lifton, R. J. *History and Human Survival*. New York: Random House, 1970.

Loewenstein, R. M.; Newman, L. M.; Schur, M.; and Solnit, A., eds. *Psychoanalysis, A General Psychology*. New York: International Universities Press, 1966.

Lorenz, K. "Ritualization in the psychosocial evolution of human culture." In: Sir Julian Huxley, ed. *Philosophical Transactions of the Royal Society of London*. Series B, no. 172, vol. 251, 1966.

——*Die Ruckseite des Spiegels*. Munich: R. Piper & Co., 1973.

Neubauer, P. B. "The life cycle as indicated by the nature of the transference in the psychoanalysis of children." *International Journal of Psycho-Analysis* 61 (1980): 137–43.

Piaget, J. "The general problems of the psychobiological development of the child." In *Discussions on Child Development*. Vol. IV, edited by Tanner, Jr., and B. Inhelder, pp. 3–27. New York, International Universities Press, 1960.

Spitz, R. A. "Life and the dialogue." In *Counterpoint: Libidinal Object and Subject*, edited by H. S. Gaskill. New York: International Universities Press, 1963.

Stockard, C. H. *The Physical Basis of Personality*. New York: W.W. Norton, 1931.

Tucker, R. C. *Philosophy and Myth in Karl Marx*. London & New York: Cambridge University Press, 1961.